Praise for *Fearless Conversations School Leaders Have to Have*

Fearless Conversations School Leaders Have to Have *is a necessary read for any school leader seeking to learn how to use strong educational principles in order to reach academic excellence on a global scale. The authors expertly describe the methods that will create a motivational learning environment for the entire school community.*

Allison Tennyson-Ibrahim, M.Ed., Principal
American Creativity Academy
Kuwait

Fearless Conversations School Leaders Have to Have *is a professional "toolbox" for aspiring as well as experienced school administrators and teacher leaders or any educator who cares about meeting the needs of today's student. Drs. Jones and Blake have provided a book that is clear and engaging. It is loaded with real-world advice. How to address difficult issues in a leadership role, for example, is presented in a realistic perspective through real-life examples, vignettes, and personal reflections that come not only from the authors themselves but also from school leaders currently in the field. These proven strategies bring credibility to the authors' work. I highly recommend this book. It is a practical guide that can help school leaders stay on the forefront of success in their schools.*

Linda Pincham, Associate Professor
Roosevelt University
Chicago, Illinois

The title of this book, Fearless Conversations School Leaders Have to Have, *invites educators at all levels of school reform to follow the authors on an authentic journey toward moral and ethical harmony while discovering best practices for teaching and learning alike.*

The core principles of each of the seven chapters convey an inspirational repertoire of school improvement designs, strategies, organizational tools, and reflections. Any supervisor can utilize these principles when leading school and/or organizational transformation. The authors' use of humor to illustrate the intricacies of engaging in powerful conversations in formal and informal contexts offers opportunities to better understand differing perspectives.

Deborah R. Jackson, **Former President (2015)**
Learning Forward, Inc.
Oxford, Ohio

Fearless Conversations School Leaders Have to Have *is the kind of book principals are eager to devour, especially those new to the profession. Jones and Blake share powerful insights and provide real-life fearless leadership examples and non-examples that can help to shape a principal's leadership vision. Their awareness of the challenges and opportunities principals face when they walk through the doors of their schools every day makes this book a must-have. As a new teacher who was under Dr. Blake's leadership almost 20 years ago, I can say with certainty that she has walked her talk and has a way of mentoring and guiding that is real, relevant, and learner-centered, even if that learner is an adult. I can't wait to share this book with the principals I lead!*

Natalie Grayson, **Supervisor**
Columbus City Schools
Columbus, Ohio

Filled with practical suggestions and reflective opportunities, this relevant and comprehensive book provides an excellent resource for active school administrators or students in training to be school administrators. With a focus on all practitioners, the authors, using clear and concrete examples, have provided a basis for understanding topics related to the profession. This book provides valuable insights and perspective from two proven leaders and should be required reading for certification courses.

Roberto A. Pamas, EdD, **Associate Professor—Education Leadership**
George Mason University
Fairfax, Virginia

Given how quickly our increasingly diverse world is changing, there are few more urgent challenges than engaging leaders in effective communication strategies that build functional relationships that transform schools and education systems. Fearless Conversations School Leaders Have to Have *is seasoned with scenarios that all leaders will undoubtedly encounter in their leadership journey, and provides practical guidelines that light the path for school leaders who are building collective school experiences for all learners. Rooted in compelling examples and coupled with engaging approaches, the book provides a blueprint for fearless communication in our increasingly diverse schools.*

Sherida Britt, Director, Learning Solutions and Services
Association for Supervision and Curriculum Development (ASCD)
Alexandria, Virginia

This book is timely, practical, and clearly anchored in the rich leadership and coaching experiences of the writers. It's a must read for all leaders and aspiring leaders at the building and central office level and will also be useful at the university level where new leaders are being prepared and inspired.

Lynda C. Wood, Ed.D, Retired Superintendent
Southfield Public School District
Southfield, Michigan

This book is a treasure trove of great advice, anecdotes, and wisdom from two highly successful principals and educational leaders. It will be especially useful to new administrators confronting the challenges and powerful opportunities present in schools today, especially urban centers characterized by diversity, rising expectations, and diminishing resources.

John L. Brown, Ph.D., Executive Director of
Curriculum Design and Services
Alexandria City Public Schools
Alexandria, Virginia

I am enthusiastic about Jones' and Blake's book, Fearless Conversations School Leaders Have to Have. *I have witnessed many times in group settings Jones' inclusive, thought provoking, and intellectually stimulating manner in ensuring that we arrive at creative and effective solutions. And I know this is born out of his 25 years of success in the educational arena. He has been recognized as the Outstanding High School Principal in Virginia and NASSP/MetLife National Principal of the Year and a much sought after educational consultant. So the ideas he shares in this book with his colleague, Vera Blake, are truly worth examining to ensure our young people are fully prepared for work and life in the 21st century.*

James Brown, Network Broadcaster
CBS Sports & CBS News
Baltimore, Maryland

*Irving C. Jones, Sr., and Vera Blake guide readers along the path to thoughtful educa-
tion reform in* Fearless Conversations School Leaders Have to Have. *With years
of invaluable school leadership as their foundation, these nationally-acclaimed
school leaders and professional learning experts share how the importance of common visions, distributed leadership, and attention to adult and student learning in
context can make a significant difference along the route to college and career readiness. Discovering evidence-based steps to improve student achievement throughout
this narrative, the reader is pulled into a setting replete with dedicated change-
agents who are determined to eradicate the obstacles of indifference and submission
to failure. Demonstrating that collective action is founded in the belief that all
students can soar to a life of personal fulfilment and success, Blake and Jones share
practical leadership skills and proof points that cultivate student agency through the
quality of care and development provided to educators at every level who are responsible for students' academic achievement. This is a must-read primer for leaders
looking to address the challenges of sustained success in closing fundamental gaps
in teacher development and student learning.*

Dr. Lillian M. Lowery, Vice President for P–12 Policy,
Research, and Practice
The Education Trust
Washington, DC

*Successful school leaders set the tone, climate, and culture for their teams, depart-
ments, and schools; Jones and Blake have a firm grasp on this notion and provide
effective and practical strategies for learning to accomplish this. As challenging as
educational leadership is today, Jones and Blake approach the topic with "hopeful
realism" and an understanding that fearless conversations are essential if school
leaders hope to enhance instruction, improve student results, and build capacity
among stakeholders. In* Fearless Conversations School Leaders Have to Have,
*Jones and Blake draw on their many years of successful experiences and provide
leaders and aspiring leaders with sound advice on a range of topics necessary for
helping students—including honing goals and purpose, developing relationships
with stakeholders, utilizing data, and implementing professional development.
With an eye on 21st century skills, Jones and Blake convey the urgent need for
courageous leaders to leverage these skills and others in the pursuit of continued
refinement and improvement in teams and across schools. By providing helpful
examples of schools addressing these needs as well as reflective questions to assist*

readers and leaders, Jones and Blake hit the mark on helping school leaders find a balance between good management and effective leadership.

John Gabriel, Principal of the Year
Loudoun County Schools
Ashburn, Virginia

Jones and Blake take proven strategies from the field and provide you with a structure for working and leading with the wisdom and creativity needed in our schools today. We can't build the future for our students by perfecting the past, and this book provides the compass points to follow on the journey. Our profession needs more books like this!

Raymond J. McNulty, Dean, School of Education
Southern New Hampshire University
Author of *It's Not Us Against Them: Creating The Schools We Need*
Hookset, New Hampshire

FEARLESS CONVERSATIONS SCHOOL LEADERS HAVE TO HAVE

This book is dedicated to Benson D. Blake and Jeannette G. Jones for their unwavering support, love, and encouragement from the beginning of this project to its conclusion. Their advice, suggestions, and insights were valued and appreciated as we collaborated on this endeavor.

FEARLESS CONVERSATIONS SCHOOL LEADERS HAVE TO HAVE

IRVING C. JONES, SR.
VERA BLAKE

Foreword by Bill Daggett

CORWIN
A SAGE Publishing Company

A SAGE Publishing Company

FOR INFORMATION:

Corwin

A SAGE Company

2455 Teller Road

Thousand Oaks, California 91320

(800) 233-9936

www.corwin.com

SAGE Publications Ltd.

1 Oliver's Yard

55 City Road

London, EC1Y 1SP

United Kingdom

SAGE Publications India Pvt. Ltd.

B 1/I 1 Mohan Cooperative Industrial Area

Mathura Road, New Delhi 110 044

India

SAGE Publications Asia-Pacific Pte. Ltd.

3 Church Street

#10-04 Samsung Hub

Singapore 049483

Publisher: Arnis Burvikovs

Senior Associate Editor: Desirée A. Bartlett

Editorial Assistant: Kaitlyn Irwin

Marketing Manager: Nicole Franks

Production Editor: Veronica Stapleton Hooper

Copy Editor: Pam Schroeder

Typesetter: Hurix Systems Pvt. Ltd.

Proofreader: Wendy Jo Dymond

Indexer: Molly Hall

Cover Designer: Michael Dubowe

Printed in the United States of America

ISBN: 978-1-5063-6754-5

This book is printed on acid-free paper.

17 18 19 20 21 10 9 8 7 6 5 4 3 2 1

Contents

Chapter 3: Improving Through Effective Feedback   61

Chapter 4: Increasing Parent and Community Stakeholder Partnerships   85

Foreword

Leadership in education, as in every other sector of society, has always been important. However, today that leadership is both more important and more difficult than ever before. That is why *Fearless Conversations About Leadership: How to Step Out of Your Comfort Zone and Really Help Kids* is a must read for all existing and aspiring administrators and teacher leaders.

To make this point, let me pose just one of many fearless conversations school leaders today need to lead. Today's schools were designed to prepare students for success in the 20th century—a time when students needed to have a series of skills and knowledge that schools were well organized and focused on to teach. The technology/information-based society our students will now work and live in has changed many of the skills and knowledge they will need and, most important, how they will need to be used. Much of what we have traditionally taught and tested in our schools can now be Googled. Therefore, by way of example, we won't let students use their technology when they take a test because they might Google the answer or share information with others via a text or e-mail. In other words, they might use resources or work with others—the two most basic skills needed for success in the world beyond school.

This raises one of many questions school leaders need to confront. Are we trying to make technology conform to our 20th-century schools, or are we trying to transform our 20th-century schools to better prepare our students for success in the 21st century's technology/information-based society in which they will live and work?

The authors have a rich history in helping their colleagues address difficult issues such as these. Therefore, their suggestions in this book are not theoretical; they are proven strategies. From creating an environment that will have such thoughtful and soul-searching conversations to developing a vision-driven culture to frame the discussion, the authors provide great insights and also very practical strategies.

As the authors so nicely lay out, fearless conversations can only be productive when they are thoughtfully planned and executed.

Having personally watched the authors successfully lead their schools, it is a pleasure to now see them helping existing and aspiring school leaders to also benefit from their experiences and insights.

Bill Daggett, Ed.D.

Founder and Chairman of the International Center for
Leadership in Education

Acknowledgments

Corwin gratefully acknowledges the contributions of the following reviewers:

Mary K. Culver, Clinical Professor, K–12 Educational Leadership
Arizona University
Flagstaff, Arizona

Bill Daggett, Founder and Chairman
International Center for Leadership in Education
Rexford, New York

Dr. Rich Hall, Director of Elementary Education
Henrico County Public Schools
Henrico, Virginia

Kathryn Jones, Clinical Instructor in Educational Leadership
Lamar University
Beaumont, Texas

Scott A. Miller, Middle School Educator
The American School of Kinshasa
Kinshasa, Democratic Republic of Congo

Melinda Whittle, High School Vice Principal
Arizona Preparatory Academy
Phoenix, Arizona

About the Authors

 **Dr. Irving C. Jones, Sr.**, a native son of New York City's South Bronx, spent 34 years in public education. Dr. Jones received his bachelor of arts degree from William Penn University, master's of education degree in educational administration from the University of Virginia, and his doctoral degree in educational administration and policy studies from the Virginia Polytechnic Institute and State University.

Moving through the ranks from an English teacher to a high school principal and then an executive director, Dr. Jones has initiated a variety of mentorship programs for both students and teachers and developed partnerships among private industries, community colleges, universities, and high schools. Dr. Jones has been recognized as a leader on topics of educational leadership. Over the last 25 years, Dr. Jones has presented at international, national, state, and local conferences on topics including minority student achievement, dropout prevention, interdisciplinary instruction in the secondary school, supervision of instruction, teaching strategies that engage active learning, career pathways, creating collaborative teaching and learning environments in schools, students transitioning from alternative placements, the transition of ninth graders into high school, and leadership in an age of accountability.

Dr. Jones was selected as the 2002 Outstanding High School Principal for Virginia. In October 2002 Dr. Jones was named the 2003 NASSP/MetLife National Principal of the Year. Additionally, for his dedication to education in the Commonwealth of Virginia in 2003, he was awarded the Virginia Lottery's Excellence in Education Award.

Dr. Jones since 2013 has been the president of ICJ & Associates LTD. And, since 2009, he has served as a senior consultant for the International Center for Leadership in Education, a division of Houghton Mifflin and Harcourt. Dr. Jones currently serves on the board of trustees for William Penn University, and his hobbies include singing in his church choir, martial arts, reading, crossword puzzles, motorcycling, and swimming. He is married to his high school sweetheart, Jeannette, and they have one son, 25-year-old Irving Jr.

Dr. Vera Blake, president of VJ Blake and Associates, Inc., is currently an international consultant who is working as a leadership coach and professional developer for instructional improvement. Her work has included capacity-building coaching and consulting for school improvement in schools and districts nationwide, the US Virgin Islands, Istanbul, and the Middle East. This capacity-building work has included coaching K–12 school leaders, designing curriculum and instructional improvement seminars and workshops, and working as an adviser and coach to primary decision makers at school and district levels. She has extensive experience in integrating technology in curriculum design and student engagement strategies. In addition, she served as adjunct professor at the University of Virginia, George Mason University, Virginia Tech, and the University of the District of Columbia. As a retired high school and middle school principal from Fairfax County, Virginia, with a master's degree from the University of Virginia and an Ed.D. from Vanderbilt University, she was Virginia Middle School

Principal of the Year, Fairfax County Principal of the Year, and a *Washington Post* Distinguished Educational Leader. She was also a contributing author to the book *Transforming Ourselves, Transforming Schools: Middle School Change* and a coauthor of several academic articles touching on school-community partnership, diversity, student achievement, and school management.

Introduction

Courage is not lack of fear but rather it is taking action in the face of, and despite, fear—*feel the fear and do it anyway!*

—Author Unknown

Don't be afraid to fail. Be afraid to not try.

—Author Unknown

Take on the Challenge to Make New Mistakes

This book will openly address some issues and concerns that are controversial or uncomfortable but deserve to be addressed. The majority of the ideas, advice, and solutions offered is particularly effective for leaders who may be outside their comfort zones, working in learning environments where students and families are economically challenged or academically deficient. Too many school leaders become so excited about serving in leadership positions that they do not take enough time to ensure that their skill sets are good or appropriate matches for the needs in their schools. Others begin to realize that after serving for many years in their positions, their schools changed "when they weren't looking," and their skill sets no longer fit their schools' needs.

Leaders make mistakes as do all other humans. The authors encourage readers to make some new mistakes rather than repeat those that we and others have made. Thus, much of the content of this book emerged from the lessons learned from both authors and others with whom we've worked.

To meet the needs of today's learners, fearless leadership is required to continually lead and support the adults who work with these learners. Many leaders have completed the course work, and have some practical knowledge and experiences, but still lack the essential skill sets required to move stakeholders toward progress. A challenging problem for too many leaders is how, with what, and when to collaborate well with stakeholders. Remaining politically correct, being careful not to offend, and concentrating on getting promotions or retaining a position can often cloud the focus required to strengthen a leader's effectiveness. The bottom line is that school leaders need to recognize and accept that their roles require them to be effective, perpetual, and positive change facilitators. They must remain focused upon the journey rather than a destination.

Many novice leaders experience insecurities about their leadership. Their own perceptions range from a lack of overall confidence to the very real fear of being "burned" for making wrong decisions. Combining more than 40 years of administrative experience, the authors have navigated and continue to work with countless others who have successfully "sailed the same seas." The more important issue is not to try to avoid mistakes as much as it is to have a commitment to always learn something from each error.

> A leader takes people where they want to go. A great leader takes people where they don't necessarily want to go but ought to be.
>
> —Rosalyn Carter

Factors Required for Fearless Leadership

It takes courage and a strong sense of self-knowledge to lead change and plan for change. A personal commitment to "hang in there" is essential to move forward, even when the going gets tough and the journey is rougher or longer than anticipated. It is our belief that those change leaders who sustain their beliefs that efforts to ensure progress for all children, who keep students first in all endeavors, are rewarded with high student achievement.

It is also our belief that much of what we know about improving learning opportunities and access to a better education for students in classrooms should also be applied to leading and managing the adults who are responsible for their achievements. In 2003, Robert Marzano published *What Works in Schools (WWIS): Translating Research Into Action;* in 1995 Carol Tomlinson published the first edition of *How to Differentiate Instruction in Mixed-Ability Classrooms;* and in 1998 Jay McTighe and Grant Wiggins published the first edition of *Understanding by Design.* Their findings, which comprised more than 40 years of synthesized, sound educational research, became tremendously popular mostly because of the practicality of organizing and presenting the information in a user-friendly format for widespread use by classroom teachers. These works resonated strongly with educators who were deeply involved with reform. They were popular also because they offered practical, doable ideas and solutions to ongoing issues that prior to the comprehensiveness of their work, were addressed in a more piecemeal fashion. Much of their work can also be insightful for leaders who wish to work more effectively with adult learners.

What Works in Schools (2003) condensed the research into three factors (school-, teacher-, and student-level) that could be addressed separately or collectively. The book also included analysis tools to help novice and experienced educators more effectively develop skills to improve student achievement outcomes. When we apply these factors to adult stakeholders in schools, they are equally as effective in improving outcomes and goals.

The school-level factors as applied to school faculties should be examined as implementing guaranteed and viable work environment; conquering challenging goals and providing effective feedback; creating effective parent partnerships and community involvement; sustaining a safe, productive, and organized work environment; and encouraging and enriching collegiality and focusing on professional development. The common thread that pulls these factors together is the need for strong, courageous, collaborative communications that becomes the focal point of all school leadership activities and that fosters and promotes continuous student achievement.

Lessons from the teacher-level factors that apply to strong leadership include those that impact job satisfaction and performance. The impact on teachers based upon the decisions and choices that are made by leaders include those that affect the physical and emotional environment, their sense of efficacy and empowerment, and deliberate recognition of the importance of their work (from Ken Blanchard and Sheldon Bowles's *Gung Ho* [1997]).

Student-level factors lead us to think about the inclusion and involvement of students, parents, and community stakeholders and their importance in impacting greater student achievement. Recognizing the differences between including and involving stakeholders in schooling and ensuring a balance of both concepts is often the prerogative of school leaders and frequently is underutilized for maximum effect. When those distinctions are not accurately addressed, opportunities for growth are lost.

In *Understanding by Design* McTighe and Wiggins (1998) provided adaptable tools that allowed focused planning for success and that included ways to generate greater buy-in from the stakeholders. McTighe taught us to remain focused on intended outcomes and planning and continuously check to ensure that we stay on track to achieve or exceed the stated goals as we begin and make progress with the desired results in mind. Again, when school leaders apply the principles of understanding by design when working with teachers, they can experience more success resulting in greater achievement for students.

Today's leaders must have a clear vision of the big picture, including everyone's roles and contributions to the organization. These leaders must visibly support faculties in ways other than those that are traditional or comfortable. Understanding the differences between equality and equity and thoughtfully applying both concepts appropriately are often more important than strictly following past protocols and expectations. Leaders need to develop and strengthen strong organizational skills, take time to ensure that they remain fully apprised of current trends and research, and at the same time utilize that information to motivate, lead, and inspire all stakeholders.

Closer examination of these concepts offers powerful clues to improve schools and student outcomes by applying them to leading adult stakeholders. It will be beneficial for reformists to emphasize one or more of the following ideas and suggestions: create and sustain a viable work environment; craft and conquer strong missions and visions by effective feedback; explore effective strategies to include parent and community stakeholders; manage and sustain an organized, productive, and ever-changing school culture; boost collegial climates by providing embedded professional development; and plan to make a positive difference. These ideas are particularly intriguing when reflecting upon the needs of novice leaders and for experienced leaders who need to broaden their repertoires.

Audience

In this book we primarily address the needs of central office supervisors, school administrators, aspiring administrators, teacher leaders, and community leaders. It is our hope that the guidance we provide will assist school leaders in recognizing and putting to use those strategies that will empower and support staffs to work at their full potential, build trust, and strengthen collegiality.

Goals

Our goal is provide strategies that will engage school leaders, teachers, students, and community members to invest in fearless and collaborative communication and to improve the academic

achievement of all students. More importantly, this book will provide doable, practical ideas and strategies that can be put to use
immediately in a user-friendly format to address individual and
collective needs of district leaders, school leaders, and community
leaders to support students and adults.

Strong, courageous, focused, collaborative leadership that is
anchored in credible research is a win–win approach for all stakeholders. Within most organizations and relationships, communication is a major key to success. We will share vignettes and
examples from a variety of experiences that may be relevant to
other school leaders and that will ignite additional thinking and
ideas that will facilitate greater achievement for all students. We
will discuss strategies that move school leaders from more traditional methodologies toward stronger transformational leadership. The vignettes, examples, and professional experiences are
shared to illustrate effective practices. We invite readers to share
their personal experiences with us.

This book aims to offer a range of tools for readers including the
following:

- Lessons that present ideas of things that can be done

- Examples of mistakes to avoid

- Ideas that may spark a note of controversy for some
  leaders

- Ideas that resonate strongly

- Commonsense approaches to common problems school
  leaders face

We believe that if real progress is to be made, it is time to take calculated, research-based risks. School leaders who embrace change
keep students first in all endeavors, and believe in themselves, will
experience success they never thought possible. In this book you
will find examples of the positive impact this can have on student
achievement.

We offer a fresh approach to reflect upon and make sustainable changes that can result in stronger achievement for students. Leadership courage must be calculated, anchored, and applied using the best available research. In addition it is essential that leaders focus on collaboration, cooperation, and their passion for the work and the students who they serve each and every day. It is a book that illustrates how to improve in an ongoing way with minimum stress or additional expenses. Ideas, suggestions, and examples provided will validate, spark new twists, and provide deeper insights on addressing existing, unforeseen, and developing challenges.

Why Read This Book?

There are several unique and compelling reasons why this book is important and contributes to developing stronger and better leadership:

- The book can be used as a handbook or practical how-to guide to build and strengthen leadership capacity among stakeholders in schools and systems.

- The book also empowers aspiring and experienced leaders to facilitate ongoing changes to perpetually improve learning opportunities for students, teachers, and other stakeholders.

- The contents help generate ideas and solutions for many dilemmas that have to be addressed by today's school leaders. In addition the book includes vignettes and examples that feature relevant and doable ideas and strategies that can easily be replicated.

The ideas presented are useful and doable and do not require additional funding to implement. Some of the suggestions can replace or enhance current practices and routines.

Thus, leaders who reflect on the contents of this book can become more efficient and effective, lead change, and mobilize a community to support the initiatives of the school.

Finally, this book offers practical and creative ideas that either help resolve issues or validate the choices that less experienced leaders can or should make. Newly identified school leaders often feel isolated and perform their duties without adequate support; they are less likely to make creative decisions when they are unsure about their support. Some of the strategies presented in this book are also ones that busy leaders may not have had opportunities to explore. Too often when difficulties appear, many are encouraged to stay within expected protocols, even though there is little confidence that these protocols have been highly successful during the recent past.

It is the hope of the authors that school leaders begin to see their roles through a new lens that embraces change and innovation. It is only through collaborative efforts that the best thinking of all stakeholders comes forward. To operate in a manner of conducting "business as usual" is outdated and dooms schools and school districts to repeated failure. As you read this book, think about the preferred future of your school or school district and what individuals need to do to make the changes needed to move forward.

Chapter 1

Creating and Sustaining a Viable Work Environment

> Far and away the best prize that life offers is the chance to work hard at work worth doing.
>
> —Theodore Roosevelt

SPOTLIGHT ON EFFECTIVE PRACTICE: FAIR IS NOT ALWAYS EQUAL

A middle school principal in a rural setting had been working at the school for four years and had cleaned up several serious teacher attendance problems that ranged from absenteeism to teachers chronically arriving to work late. She strictly enforced attendance rules for all faculty and staff that required everyone except the evening cleaning crew to be at work by 7:30 a.m. At the beginning of her fifth

(Continued)

(Continued)

year, three teachers individually approached the principal requesting permission to arrive at school an hour later than all other teachers. Two other teachers were still on probation for chronic tardiness.

One teacher made the request because she lived more than a two-hour drive from school on a farm and, in addition to early-morning chores, felt it was a personal hardship to have to be at work at 7:30 a.m. when her classes did not begin until 9:00 a.m. Another teacher, a single mom, made the request because her children were newly enrolled in the location's best day care facility; she couldn't drop them off until 7:00 a.m., and the middle school was an hour away from that location. The third teacher made the request because she and her personal physician had determined that the early morning hours added a level of stress to her that impacted her ability to perform her best teaching.

The principal quickly involved the human resources department to ensure that district policy was followed and was not in conflict with any of the resolutions. After communicating with the assistant superintendent and an elementary principal, the first teacher who had farm chores was offered an opportunity to trade jobs with a sixth-grade teacher at the elementary school who wanted a transfer to the middle school.

The second teacher was offered an adjusted contract to perform additional duties until 5:30 p.m., which would allow her to arrive at 8:00 a.m. and pick up her children before the day care facility closed at 6:30 p.m. She was assigned the management of two after-school programs for tutoring and mentoring identified students in need. This resulted in increased and improved achievement for more than 50 students.

The third teacher was provided the option of further examination by a district-approved physician and psychiatrist or counseling to help her improve her job performance. She was also placed in the evaluation cycle two years ahead of schedule to allow the principal the opportunity to more accurately assess and coach her job performance. Ultimately, the integrity of the principal's expectations for all faculty and staff to report to work on time was maintained.

It is common knowledge among many school leaders that providing all students equitable, not just equal, access to high-quality curriculum is a challenge that is faced by all levels of educators. Sometimes the greatest problems are that many educators do not distinguish between *equitable* and *equal,* and many educators do not share the same definition of *viable curriculum.* Marzano (2003) describes *viable curriculum* as content that is shared with students that they have sufficient time to learn. When these concepts are applied to the work environment for educational stakeholders, the same needs are held by the staff.

The terms *equitable* and *equal* are not interchangeable and, when applied to the concept of educational access, should be clarified for all stakeholders. Perhaps it is best summarized by Rick Wormeli (2006) when he applied this concept to students' evaluation in the title and contents of his book *Fair Is Not Always Equal.* This concept is articulated well in making the case that although it is easier to ensure equality, it often requires deeper thinking and more work to ensure equity, particularly when applied to ideas such as opportunities and access. Much professional and excellent judgment is required to get it right for all students, and the same is equally true for adult stakeholders who work with them.

> *The terms equitable and equal are not interchangeable . . . although it is easier to ensure equality, it often requires deeper thinking and more work to ensure equity, particularly when applied to ideas such as opportunities and access.*

A viable curriculum that is presented in ways that allow students to access and master the content may become less challenging as we refine Common Core curriculums and as educators continue to explore the philosophy of differentiating instruction. Common Core curriculum helps continue to clarify what needs to be learned and, thus, helps address many of the current problems in many classrooms that feature too many goals and standards to address.

Differentiating the instruction provides faculty members with much needed support in delivery of the content in ways that are accessible to a broader range of learners. When applied to faculty members, a viable work environment requires leadership that can apply the same principles to the adult learners in a school or district. Sometimes that leadership must differentiate to address employee needs yet remain in compliance with district policies and expectations.

Although we completely agree with Marzano's (2003) premise that all students should have access to a "viable curriculum," we would go another step to focus on staff who are responsible for ensuring that students are learning. We believe strongly that in addition to students, all staff must have an equitable and viable opportunity to learn (OTL). Thus, a viable work environment for adults in schools must feature opportunities for them to learn and grow in their work environments.

As most of us are familiar with concepts and strategies regarding job-embedded learning, many are not clear on how to create or sustain the concept. A means of establishing a viable option of delivering professional development in schools is to first develop teacher leaders (TLs). Through TLs some of the more powerful learning opportunities for the entire staff can occur. The first challenge is in identifying the most effective staff members as TLs.

Instead of choosing the teacher leadership from among "volunteers," or teachers who are friendly toward the administration, or teachers who need help, better criteria for identifying these leaders could be among the following look-fors: (1) Look for those among the staff (teachers, paraprofessionals, and support personnel) who have the respect of their colleagues for their innovative, strong, and effective teaching repertoire. (2) Look for those who are working hard rather than those who are hardly working, but they are just popular for other reasons. (3) Look for those who are passionate quietly or otherwise about making a positive difference for the vision or big-picture goals of the school; their interests are beyond their scope of responsibilities. (4) Look for those who may have or who can develop hope and a positive attitude toward making changes. (5) Look for those who may not always agree with some of your perspectives, but they care intensely about the students. (6) Look for those who either are or can grow beyond the "it's not my job" syndrome. (7) Look for those who have or are capable of developing a sense of ownership for the success of the entire school.

TLs can play vital roles in creating and sustaining ongoing, job-embedded professional development. This is an opportunity for school administrators to get out of their own way, strengthen trust among the faculty, and lead their schools beyond their individual skills and perspectives.

Adult Learning

SPOTLIGHT ON EFFECTIVE PRACTICE: TEACHER LEADERS AS KEYS TO SUSTAINING A VIABLE WORK ENVIRONMENT

A middle school principal asked her team and department leaders to create a joint subcommittee for the purpose of creating a new master schedule that would feature job-embedded learning opportunities for the faculty. She provided them with resources that included attending a conference that included consultants who wrote books and articles on middle school scheduling, books, articles, and opportunities to visit several schools that featured different kinds of blocked scheduling and that featured faculty learning opportunities during their workday.

The TLs worked diligently and collaborated with their colleagues on multiple concerns to develop a master schedule that addressed the major concerns of their colleagues and achieved the goals of their mission. After two months of diligent study, research, and collaboration, they presented their recommended options to the entire faculty. Their work was applauded, approved, and implemented the following school year.

In too many schools, insufficient energy, time, and resources are invested to ensure that all staff have an OTL, and in fact, some of the support staff's growth needs are ignored while there is a high sense of urgency to improve student outcomes. It is absurd to expect teachers and other responsible staff to achieve different results with students without appropriate investment in the learning opportunities for the adults who work with them. The double-speaking dysfunctional politics that lead school decision makers to eliminate or minimize the resources and support systems that nurture and sustain opportunities for the adults to learn fly in the face of common sense and all that is known about improving schools.

On the other hand, many successful initiatives that support and provide opportunities for the adults at schools to learn often do not require significant additional funding to maintain and sustain. Sometimes it is a matter of using the resources that are available more efficiently and effectively. Often it requires courage and willingness to buck traditions to try new, innovative, and creative ideas.

One example that comes to mind is better use of the already budgeted time that many schools have for faculty, team, grade-level, departmental, and other meetings. In some school districts, school board policy requires that each school features ongoing, often monthly, faculty meetings. In most of the schools, the principal establishes a consistent day of the month and time for the meetings to be held. Each month, staff members drag themselves and colleagues to the dreaded meeting, where the principal performs as a talking head for approximately one hour, and then everyone is released and relieved until the next month.

Much of what the principal conveyed could have been delivered through another more efficient and perhaps equally as effective way. One suggestion is to make the announcements in writing using any one of several choices via a link that could be titled "Principal's Corner," or something similar, on the school's intranet. Another suggestion is to consider various ways to use available technology through voice and/or video recordings or recorded webinars that can be done while reviewing the information at one's desk.

In addition, there are multiple free websites such as Blackboard Connect. Messages can be sent from the division level and/or the school level. Schools can personalize communications such as tweets for parents to address emergency and priority matters. Messages can be used routinely at the division level for school closures, early dismissals, and announcements that are relevant to all stakeholders. It should be noted that the frequency of sharing this information using these options is beneficial when they are well publicized and promote a sense of routineness for accessing it.

An important step for principals and other administrators is to get out of their own way. What we mean by this is to take a step back and trust that as TLs, these professionals have skills that may be different but that are equally as viable as the training and background experiences that the administrative leaders have had. Strengthening the arts of silence, listening, and/or wait time will frequently prompt others to speak up and, at a sometimes surprising rate, take charge during meetings. Voilà—collaboration is born or strengthened. The more frequently this is done, the more confidence is gained and strengthened among those who have less experience as leaders. Although it is not easy, leaders often learn to become more effective by taking a backseat more often. Someone once said that good leaders are first good followers.

For example, prepare the TLs for a meeting by sharing pertinent agenda items in advance and requesting that everyone who is attending bring two potential ideas, solutions, and/or suggestions with them from themselves and/or the people they represent. This provides insights on the type of leadership qualities and skills these leaders already have as well as generating a greater sense of ownership for solutions to issues.

This simple strategy is also important to sharing the decision-making within the organization.

All input should be welcomed and considered.

An alternative use of faculty meeting time would serve student achievement and adult morale better through the delivery of quality, concise, and focused professional development during the session. This provides excellent opportunities for teacher and administrative leaders to demonstrate, model for, and teach their colleagues. For example, when there is a schoolwide focus on literacy, each monthly faculty meeting could feature TLs teaching and modeling specific literacy strategies that have proved successful across disciplines and grade levels. These meetings then become OTLs for the faculty. Similar strategies could be shared in team meetings, departmental meetings, and/or grade-level meetings.

A follow-up step is for school administrators to learn to wear the cheerleader/helper hat more effectively. This is an opportunity for additional growth for other leaders within the building in a role that is not practiced often enough. Develop stronger skills as a researcher, resource procurer, coach, and follower to support the TLs' ideas and planning.

SPOTLIGHT ON EFFECTIVE PRACTICE: TEACHERS AS LEADERS OF LEARNING

An example of what can happen in a high school of more than 130 faculty members when all three steps are followed is a more useful learning opportunity for an entire faculty. This began when one of the identified TLs approached the principal with the idea that faculty meetings could be more useful if the principal were no longer in charge. The result, after much discussion, was a unique faculty learning experience. The principal began by putting the most routine announcements that were usually made during the faculty meeting on the schoolwide intranet. Thus the principal's role during the scheduled monthly mandatory faculty meeting was minimized to opening the meeting, succinctly articulating any policy issues and ensuring that the meeting session was stocked with great food (more about that later). Make faculty meetings announcement-free zones in which all administrative announcements are relegated to paper, or e-mail, and all faculty meeting times are focused on professional sharing (Reeves, 2008).

The TLs took charge of the remainder of the time of the meetings, which were then referred to by everyone as OTLs. They established a schedule of the meetings that included which leaders would be in charge, organized by pairs, triads, or quads, to facilitate the session. They surveyed the faculty to determine what their colleagues wanted and needed to learn that would help them do a more effective job with students. Some of the feedback that was received included how to address literacy skills in subject content, how to address multiple intelligences or learning styles in the classroom, how to differentiate instruction among diverse learners, and how to use assessments and evaluations to improve instruction.

To prepare for the meetings, the group studied adult learning needs, staff development models, and delivery strategies. In addition they studied educational changes, accountability, responsibility, and ethics. They then divided the topics for each OTL and in small groups, developed lesson plans, brought the plans to a group meeting, critiqued the plans, and prepared to teach their colleagues. There was amazement at the 98 percent positive feedback from the anonymous evaluations and the 97 percent requests for more of these learning sessions that came from the faculty. One of the results was adjustments within the school's master schedule for the following year that allowed for professional development to be built into the school day for all faculty members.

Better use of time to provide learning opportunities for faculty is half of the idea. The other half is ensuring that the information that was taught in OTLs is actually used in classrooms. Yes, we mean accountability. A team approach to accountability for using and refining the support to teachers is critical. TLs and administrators can serve in extraordinary roles of meaningful, useful, and nonevaluative follow-up support to teachers.

Principals' Roles

One example is the monitoring of lesson unit designs and plans and providing feedback to teachers. Encouraging teachers to develop plans for units of study and then extracting daily work from the larger amount of that content is efficient and effective on many levels. Planning in chunks allows teachers to remain more focused on the big picture, on standards, and helps them be better prepared to address learning obstacles. TL support in reviewing these plans is nonevaluative and supportive of good instruction and helps TLs expand their expertise. Leaders should review plans of colleagues to ensure that professional development that was provided is reflected in the plans and thus used to benefit student learning. The simple use of e-mails, intranet links, and other technological tools help improve the efficiency of sharing plans and feedback about the plans. Without this accountability, the professional development sessions may not have maximum benefits or may not be worth the investment.

Another benefit to implementing this accountability process has the added benefit of allowing the TLs and administrators to support teacher leaders in coaching roles. Whereas reviewing the lesson designs and providing feedback to teachers helps ensure that instruction is aligned with the standards, it is very important that teachers have support to continually improve their skills and that multiple stakeholders remain involved with providing a high quality of education.

It is important to ensure that the announcements on the intranet are read. There are numerous electronic options that can provide information on links visited and/or e-mail reminders that are read, received, and opened. Many of us recall that a great perk to meetings, particularly those held after the school day, is the quality snacks or food. Regarding the ordering of food requests in many school communities, there are numerous organizations, small and larger businesses, that are happy to support an endeavor that ultimately benefits children by providing snacks to full meals for learning sessions. Coaches and single teachers are often especially appreciative of these supportive gestures. It is fairly easy to create a grid of weekly schedules to organize and monitor the groups, individuals, and businesses who contribute.

Supplementing and supporting OTLs is crucially important. One way is to provide incentives and recognition for efforts and progress. Some of the better incentives do not require additional funds. For example, public recognition and certificates issued during any assembly, meeting, or gathering and short paragraphs of congratulations in school publications can go a long way toward providing appropriate and meaningful recognition. Local community stakeholders often welcome an opportunity to support our efforts to improve through gift certificates. Even something as simple as the principal cooking or catering a lunch or dinner for the honorees is appreciated (unless, of course, the principal can't cook). People need to know that they are valued, that their work is recognized and appreciated, and they generally need motivation to continue to learn and grow as a priority among all that is required of them. Local stakeholders who provide support have the same needs to extend appreciation and recognition to the people who are doing their best for the community's children.

> *Public recognition issued during any gathering and short paragraphs of congratulations in school publications can go a long way toward providing meaningful recognition.*

Supporting Opportunities to Learn at Work

Another way to supplement and support OTLs is to provide growth opportunities to TLs who provide support for good instruction. For example, TLs who facilitate OTLs and provide professional development options to their colleagues are worth their weight in gold.

Providing them additional and sometimes creative ways to continue their own growth or to recognize their contributions is usually of value to them. Again, some of the better ideas do not have to require additional funding. Ideas that have been successful can include coveted parking spaces, prime real estate in the form of classroom locations, and so on. However, choosing to apply some resources in their learning is a good investment for the school and district. An effective one that we used was the strengthening and upgrading of the professional library on-site and providing incentives for staff members to use it.

Setting the stage for OTLs to become functional features of a school culture and thus supporting a viable working environment begins with trust. The first step to developing a trusting environment is for open communication to be welcomed and nurtured.

Here is how one principal accomplished this task.

SPOTLIGHT ON EFFECTIVE PRACTICE: TEACHERS VOICES NEED TO BE HEARD

Beginning the school year as the new principal in a high school, the principal was anxious to meet his entire staff at the first faculty meeting. He had an agenda prepared that included introductions and announcements for the opening day of school, a review of the school policies and procedures, expectations for student behavior and achievement, and a list of generic opening school issues. An hour had passed during this meeting when he finally asked teachers if they had any questions. To his surprise there were none; instead, there seemed to be an undercurrent of murmuring as he dismissed the teachers to return to their classrooms to get ready for the opening on the following day. One teacher stayed behind and said to him, "Teachers need a voice."

That evening the principal became concerned that he may have started off on the wrong foot. The teachers were getting what they had always received at their faculty meetings, and yet they may have left the meeting feeling that they did not have a voice. This was troubling to him. He decided that on the following day, at the scheduled end of the first day of school, the faculty meeting would be different. He took an hour to reflect upon the previous day's meeting and made a short list of items that he needed to address. He was now ready for his next meeting with teachers and staff.

At 3:00 p.m. the bell rang, and by 3:20 p.m. all teachers and staff members assembled in the auditorium. The principal began the meeting by thanking all for a very good first day. He stated that all 1,000-plus students, with the exception of 10 had their schedules correct, teachers were visible between each class change, assisting students who were new to the school, and it was one of the most successful school openings he had experienced in his 16 years as a school administrator. He then apologized for not planning an opportunity to hear their concerns on the previous day. With that one statement, the mood of the room visibly became more relaxed than that of the previous day. He noticed the smile on the face of the teacher who brought this issue to his attention. It became evident that teachers had a lot to say and needed an open invitation to do so.

To his surprise, suddenly teachers began to ask questions and talk about their previous experiences with their principals and other school leaders, both good and bad. They talked openly about some of their concerns about the abilities of many of their students, and as they talked, the principal took notes. It seemed that once the flood door opened, it wouldn't close. Interestingly enough, this didn't become a gripe session as teachers had some very legitimate concerns and made an effort to articulate them in positive and succinct ways for approximately 25 minutes. To assure them that they were heard and understood, he recorded their comments on chart paper for all to see and verify. The primary concerns were student behavior, administrative support, academic achievement, and student safety.

The principal then requested one volunteer along with the department chair of each department to prioritize the items on the list and create two questions or suggestions regarding how they could collaborate as a school faculty and staff to address these issues. They reached a unanimous decision to follow through and agreed to make a presentation at the next faculty meeting.

Incorporating teachers' voices to increase their effectiveness in a sustainable and viable work environment is critical and ensures that access for all teachers is equitable and differentiated to meet their needs. An important way to ensure the improvement of student achievement is to ensure that the faculty has timely and high-quality professional development. Providing this support helps make the increasing accountability fairer and more reasonable as it reduces the commonly observed practice of victimizing and blaming teachers for the lack of increasing achievement results for students who arrive at schools with less than optimal background skills or knowledge. To expand the knowledge base of your teachers and to intentionally engage them in their own learning, leaders must encourage them to lead the professional development initiatives in their schools.

Lessons Learned—LRD

1. **Listen** carefully and visually observe the mood of your faculty and staff audience.

2. **Reflect** upon what could be done to improve communications by allowing teachers to have a voice.

3. **Develop** a strategy or strategies for administrators and teachers to follow up on actions to be taken to move forward with a plan.

For principal leaders it is essential that administrators are perceived as good listeners. The more good listening skills are practiced, the more that is learned by a leader in the school environment. There will be times where you really don't want to hear something or someone, and those are the times when your listening skills are most needed. Ultimately at the end of the day, the principal still is the primary decision maker and has the ultimate accountability. However, if one has the habit of shutting people down when not in agreement or simply doesn't want to hear what another has to say, an environment is created where people will not trust, or they may feel that their opinions do not matter, thus reinforcing an environment where it's "them and us."

Many good leaders will acknowledge that reflective practices save them from repeating the same mistakes. Reflective practices also assist leaders in planning next steps and in managing difficult situations or situations in which the individual leader evaluates his or her own behavior. Most important, daily reflection helps a leader clear his or her mind and reduces stress. An effective leader needs to ensure that he or she has time for reflective practices every day. The following questions are a few that can guide school leaders, faculty, and staff to improve their daily work:

Reflections Prompts to Improve Daily Work

1. What was most successful today? Why?

2. What's my evidence?

3. What could I have done better today? How?

4. What can I cross off my list of things to do?

5. Did I listen to others' concerns and respond appropriately? If so, where? If not, what can I do to appropriately address their concerns?

6. How did I improve the quality of learning for my students and staff today?

7. What is a priority for tomorrow that will improve or support student learning?

Both administrators and TLs need to develop reflective practices individually, with a colleague, and in small groups. At the same time, along with reflective practices, educators should habitually develop and utilize researched-based strategies to solve some of the issues that are identified as a result of these practices.

Reflection is instrumental mediation of action and is a process that leads to thoughtful, mediated action, frequently involving the utilization and implementation of research findings and theoretical formulations of education (Clift, Houston, & Pugach, 1990). From this perspective, the purpose of reflection is instrumental in that the reflective process is used to help leaders replicate, adapt, and improve upon practices that empirical research has found to be effective. Another benefit of continuous reflective practices among administrators and staffs is that these behaviors help promote a collegial school environment. Bosher and Hazlewood defined collegiality as "a form of social organization based on shared and equal participation by all of its members" (2008, p. 69). It implies collective responsibility and describes a group of people united in a common purpose who have respect for each other's perspectives, insights and abilities in working toward that purpose. This is a foundation of a strong school culture that features a viable work environment.

SPOTLIGHT ON EFFECTIVE PRACTICE: TEACHER LEADERS TAKE THE LEAD

At a regularly scheduled faculty meeting, the principal introduced the team of teacher volunteers who agreed to present the concerns expressed by their colleagues in their departments.

They placed their concerns on chart paper in the same order from the previous meeting:

1. Student Behavior

2. Administrative Support

3. Academic Achievement

4. Student Safety

These leaders fielded questions from their colleagues that sparked a great discussion. They facilitated the dialogue among teachers and the administrative staff that resulted in a new sheet of chart paper with the same items in prioritized order:

1. Academic Achievement
2. Student Safety
3. Administrative Support
4. Student behavior

They explained the rationale for this order, and of course, everyone expressed appreciation that academic achievement was the highest priority item. It was the consensus of the teachers and staff members that the focus remain on the academic achievement of all students and that the school serve as a significant physical, emotional, and psychological safe haven in the lives of its students. An important and unified commitment emerged as teachers wanted definitions and clarifications of their individual and collective roles and the roles of the members on the administrative team.

This resulted in a very positive review of procedures and significant buy-in for handling disciplinary issues and being proactive before disciplinary issues occurred. Agreement was reached on how infractions would be handled and tools and strategies discussed that placed teacher and parent intervention as first steps. Clarification was engendered regarding roles, responsibilities, and the subsequent steps of faculty and administrative intervention when student disciplinary issues escalated. Details were thoroughly reviewed and discussed including the design of student planning guides to use by students as hall passes. In addition to the teacher's initials documenting the time the student left the class, they also served the purpose of escalating incentives for students to always have their planning guides at school. This contributed largely to helping to maintain a safe an orderly daily school environment.

(Continued)

(Continued)

This session was extremely productive, and all applauded the efforts of the volunteers and leaders who planned and facilitated this meeting. The principal summarized the meeting by thanking all faculty and staff for their involvement and then set the stage for the next meeting by asking them to attend the next meeting prepared to further define and clarify the school mission and vision.

This essential step further ensured that the stakeholders had the same understandings of the focus that guided and defined the school's culture. Interestingly enough, rather than teachers hurrying to exit the building, they stayed and discussed their positive feelings about their involvement and their expectations for similar results at the next meeting. This strategy is powerful in developing a strong, collaborative, and collegial school climate— another foundational pillar of creating and sustaining a viable work environment for all employees.

Stretch to Grow

Leaders need to deliberately, consciously, and thoughtfully step out of their comfort zones to effectively lead. Calculated risks are essential attributes for strong leadership in many schools and districts. Yes, mistakes are a part of everyone's life, but to allow the fear of making mistakes or the paralysis of being unsure of your decisions to prevail is not conducive to growth and progress. In fact, if you have not made several mistakes, stepped on a few toes, challenged a few assumptions, and/or ticked anyone off within a month, you may not have accomplished very much or may not have been doing your job well.

These following vignettes illustrate the need for school leaders at all levels to not only ensure that other stakeholders have viable and impactful voices but that their voices are also heard. Help stakeholders understand the differences between hearing and agreeing and that understanding and agreeing are different concepts. One of the hardest lessons to master as leaders is how and when to get out of your own way. Some school leaders, superintendents, principals, assistant principals, and department chairs and other leaders often work from a position of power and control rather than creating an environment of collaboration and trust.

Fearless conversations are anchored in courage. It takes courage for school leaders to consistently leave their egos at home and come into the workplace with an open mind that invites innovation and new ideas. It takes courage to be reflective and change one's point of view when confronted with other ideas—some even better than your own. It shows courage and character when school leaders can apologize when they miss the mark or cause faculty and staff to feel excluded from making decisions that impact their day-to-day practices. When we talk about collaborative communication, it is not just what we say that sends powerful messages but what is done on a daily basis. A favorite quote from one of the authors is "More than one head is good, even if one is a cabbage head."

The behaviors of school leaders are the primary ingredients for the creation of and sustaining a viable work environment. The traits of strong school leadership at all levels is having a vision, being the center of change, and demonstrating consistency between beliefs and goals and between goals and actions. We will explore in greater detail in the next chapter the creation of a strong vision and mission. But it is important to note that school leaders must have a clear vision of the preferred future of their school. They must believe that a vision is just not looking into the present, but it is seeing into the future. It's not just having goals but having strategies to achieve them and the courage, perseverance, and determination to pursue them. It's being so convinced that you're right that other people will believe you're right too.

School leaders have to willingly be the center of change by facilitating conversations about the need for change and allowing for progressive

> *Fearless conversations are anchored in courage. It takes courage for school leaders to consistently leave their egos at home and come into the workplace with an open mind that invites innovation and new ideas.*

thinking around the goals established to realize the changes needed to sustain a viable work environment. For example, as school and district leaders, consider the following questions for discussions and reflection with other stakeholders.

Table 1.1

Questions	Responses	Reflections	Action to Be Taken
1. How will we communicate with each other in our workplace (both formally and informally)?			
2. How will we resolve conflicts when they occur?			
3. How do we build support and consensus around actions needed for improvement?			
4. What do we mean when we say, as a community, that we have high expectations for all students?			
5. What are our expectations for each other regarding professional demeanor and decorum in the workplace?			

Leading Change

This is a good starting place for leaders who strive to lead change in their schools and districts by setting the stage for creating and sustaining a viable work environment. Record the responses (assign a recorder), and generate ideas as a group. These questions create a forum for school leaders to communicate to stakeholders and staff what it is that he or she believes. It is important that these conversations occur to ensure transparency about what the individual and collective expectations are for all.

At the beginning of the school year, during the first pre-school meeting is often a good time to facilitate this discussion. It is not only important for the school leaders to let faculties and staffs know what is believed, but it is more important for leaders to know what they believe and help all stakeholders reach agreement upon what they will work toward together.

As a group of leaders, reflect upon the responses, and try to categorize them in priority order. Develop action steps to create the workplace that all can agree upon to achieve stated goals, prioritizing them for address and resolving. Especially important is to develop a means to evaluate and assess progress and achieved results. Be sure to build in benchmarks to monitor progress.

As school leaders develop it is important to demonstrate consistency between beliefs and goals at all times. In other words, if you are going to talk the talk, you have to walk the walk. Someone is always listening to what school leaders are saying to determine the degree to which their stated goals are intentional and aligned with their behaviors. For example, there are school leaders who profess to have an open-door policy but never make themselves available to discuss issues with students, faculty and staff, or parents.

Another example is the school leader who insists that teachers are visible in the hallways between class changes or during breaks but remains in his or her office during these same times. This is behavior that is inconsistent with what the school leader says he or she believes is important. The leaders have to model the behaviors they want others to emulate; "do as I say, not as I do" doesn't work.

Other traits of a strongly positive leader in creating and sustaining a viable work environment include taking risks, helping others reach their full potential, connecting to and caring about students, and talking seriously about high expectations with realistic hope. Risk taking is often very difficult for leaders who always want to play it safe.

Playing it safe may keep you under the radar of criticisms, but as a leader there will be times when you will be faced with dilemmas and conflicts that are not in the best interests of the children everyone is there to serve. There have been so many times we've wanted to say, "Stop worrying about your next promotion," or "Stop playing politics and just do the right thing instead of always trying to do things right."

SPOTLIGHT ON EFFECTIVE PRACTICE: ASKING FORGIVENESS, NOT PERMISSION

In 2001 a middle school principal was assigned to a new building in a small midwestern city. The school was in an affluent neighborhood, and it had a history of grouping students by ability. The school was well known for its science and technology program that operated under the guise of a gifted-and-talented (GT) program. The principal noticed immediately that there was a lack of diversity among the students in the GT program.

Students who were bussed in from the housing projects, mostly black and Hispanic students, were less likely to be included in the GT programs. The principal learned that students were placed in the program based on teachers' recommendations and not consistently because of their ability or any standardized criteria. Examining the data of his students, he noticed that many students who were receiving As and Bs were not being recommended into the GT program; again, the majority of these students were children of color.

In addition, the principal learned that students who were bussed into this school did not have parents who were aware of the entry requirements for the GT program, or the parents knew very little about the program. This lack of information and awareness prohibited advocacy for their children's participation in the GT program.

The principal determined that the first step in a multifaceted approach needed to address his concerns was to better educate all parents by going out into the community, holding community forums, speaking at community churches, and even going to the workplaces of some parents who could not attend meetings because of their work schedules.

As a result, more parents began to contact teachers and began asking them questions about recommending their children to the GT program. By the end of the first semester, the number of recommendations for students more than doubled at each grade level. As a next step, the principal decided to expand access to the science and technology program to include accessibility to all students in the school.

Clearly, the principal believed that this was the right thing to do, took action, and didn't ask permission from his supervisor to make all parents aware of the GT program or expand the science and technology program by making it assessable to all students in his school. Was this a reasonable risk on the part of this principal? What were the consequences of his action? Well, as you might guess, there was some resistance on the part of parents whose children were already in the GT program and thought that it would be watered down if it included all the students. And as you might also guess, there was resistance from several teachers who were anchored in the GT program and had the luxury of just teaching those students selected in the past.

(Continued)

(Continued)

Eventually, school board members became involved, and of course, the principal ultimately had to meet with the superintendent and then the board in closed sessions to explain his actions. The principal presented compelling current research on the value of mixed-ability grouping of students and made a convincing argument for the support of inherent ability of all of his students.

In addition he guaranteed that the students would show academic gains across all grade levels. The board and the superintendent supported his proposal with the provision that in the future, he must obtain permission prior to initiating actions that could result in a broad range of opposition. Of course, at the end of the next semester, the students showed gains at every level.

A key element to the success of any leader who challenges the status quo or who is seeking changes that challenge deep-seated practices already within a culture—do your homework. Anchor decisions and choices in data and credible research. It also helps if one is willing to sometimes seek forgiveness rather than permission.

The Bottom Line

A rule of thumb that the authors of this book will support is "If it is in the best interest of all students, it is the right thing to do." We've also found that when one makes an error with this intention in mind, things still usually work out for the best. In the previous vignette the principal had to make a decision that had much to do with access and equity. It might have been an easy sell to his superintendent if he approached him first, or it could have gotten killed by analysis paralysis as a committee may have been formed to analyze and study the issues for the next two years.

On a daily basis school leaders have to be cheerleaders and coaches to assist students, faculty, and staff in reaching their full potential.

In sustaining a viable working environment, it is wise to remember that members of the school community want to feel valued in whatever role they play. A school leader who pays attention to the needs of his or her community is always open to assist. Sometimes it is career counseling of teachers who may ultimately want to become school administrators. Sometimes it is just listening to teachers or students who are having problems at home with siblings, parents, or their spouses. Sometimes it is mediating conflicts between students and teachers or teachers with teachers. In the role of school leadership, you must be prepared for the unexpected.

When serving as an instructional leader, one must be prepared to assist teachers in developing lesson plans that are highly engaging, rigorous, and relevant to the learning needs of all students. It is powerful when an instructional leader will co-plan and prepare to model a lesson for teachers who need to improve their pacing and instructional delivery.

Connecting to and caring for students are primary reasons why schools exist. Our schools are oases to many students who come from homes where they don't have the support they need to be successful in their academic pursuits. This is evident in homes across the socioeconomic, ethnic, and other spectrums that exist.

School-age children spend more time with other adults (often teachers) than their own parents, and thus, it is imperative that educators are prepared to connect to the academic, social, and psychological needs of all students. Adult–student relationships and interactions are critical in schools. Although educators are fully aware of the importance of communicating seriously about high expectations for students, it is equally as vital that these expectations apply to and are communicated to faculty and staff. School leaders have the task of keeping mind-set out in front of all efforts in creating and sustaining a viable work environment, day in and day out.

This brings to mind how absolutely essential it is to include support staff such as clerical, custodial, and cafeteria workers; bus drivers;

and many others who often are less visible in schools and districts. These stakeholders are critical in creating and sustaining a viable work environment. In addition, their contributions can enhance and enrich this endeavor or not depending upon the value that is placed on their contributions. We've learned that very often staff members among this group can be some of the strongest advocates and representatives of what is valued in workplaces.

Thus, it is incumbent upon leaders to ensure that members from these groups are included in viable ways to meet their needs and increase their understandings of being considered when strengthening and enriching a viable work environment. Everything that was discussed regarding meeting the needs of faculties also pertains to this group. Frequently, undiscovered resources, talents, gifts, and contributions from support personnel remain overlooked or untapped.

SPOTLIGHT ON EFFECTIVE PRACTICE: LEADERSHIP CAN EMERGE FROM SUPPORT STAFF

When a district leadership team encouraged citizens and communities to support mentoring programs and extracurricular support for our youth, a principal determined to establish a mentoring program within her school for students Grades 6 through 8. Data indicated that 60 percent of the students were from single-parent homes, 70 percent were on free or reduced-price lunch, and there were 67 nations represented among the student population. Connecting students to strong adult role models, tutoring, and opportunities for positive dialogue would definitely benefit her students.

Every day for several weeks, she made announcements and requests seeking and hoping someone would accept the challenge and responsibility of leading this initiative. One day a member of the evening shift of custodians approached her and asked if she minded if he organized and managed a mentoring program. He'd heard the announcements, requests, and discussions and was very interested.

After receiving a positive response and encouragement from the principal, he designed a program customized for the students in that school and put together a recruitment process to attract new teachers and young professionals within the community. In addition, he researched and wrote a grant to provide funding for these interested adults so that they could avoid using personal and limited funds to treat children to bowling, movies, skating, and other activities.

The results of this program were extraordinary. Grades dramatically improved schoolwide, and classroom discipline improved. The overall school climate underwent a strongly positive change.

This particular custodian, unbeknownst to anyone at the school, had multiple college degrees from his country; was fluent in five languages and learned Spanish, Korean, and Vietnamese from coworkers; and was taking college classes to obtain a U.S. college degree as his was not recognized in this country. In addition, he worked two full-time jobs saving his money to eventually bring his wife and two children to the United States, where she earned another nursing degree, and they sent both sons to college.

Lessons learned from this experience included spending time to ensure that all staff understand and value how a viable work environment that appreciates, supports, and harvests the contributions of all staff members can enrich student life, experiences, and achievement. That experience also taught the principal how important the work environment is to all stakeholders.

Summary

In conclusion, this chapter articulates how essential it is to collaborate by having courageous conversations to create and sustain a viable work environment. It discusses the need for providing teachers with OTLs, identifying and supporting TLs, and ensuring that teachers have a voice that is heard and that they play critical roles in making needed changes. Leaders need to be intentional and deliberate in creating and sustaining a viable work environment for all stakeholders. There is no way to sugarcoat the work of school and district leaders. It is hard work every day.

Marzano's (2003) research is clear that students require a positive and strong school culture to ensure that all have access to a high-quality instructional delivery and curriculum content and that they must have sufficient time to learn this information as priorities in addressing student achievement. It is equally true that adults who work with students must have these same opportunities to learn, grow, and contribute in their work environment. The principles of this factor when applied to adult learning are the same. Often school leaders may not have sufficient awareness, time, or skills within their leadership repertoire to address building and sustaining a culture that supports and enriches adult stakeholders. It is important that teachers, custodians, secretaries, parents, and all other stakeholders also have voices in building and sustaining a high-quality learning environment that is focused on excellence on multiple levels.

When analyzing the work environment in your school and district, there are several questions that leaders should ask and answer honestly. Are fearless and courageous conversations taking place around curriculum, equality, and equity? Is the school community where it needs to be in sustaining a workplace that meets the needs of students, teachers, and the educational community at large? If not, why not? Is there a means of communication that keeps all focused on the needs of the students we serve? Is there an ongoing dialogue to make needed changes to promote progress with and for students or with and for other adults?

This chapter has provided some direction in answering these questions and perhaps prompted additional thinking that will involve developing a longer list of questions that should be answered as it pertains to the distinct culture of each school or school division. Readers are invited to share their insights, queries, and experiences with the authors.

Reflections

The following questions are designed to provoke additional thinking and discussions about creating and sustaining viable work environments in schools:

1. What learning opportunities are embedded during the workday that allow employees to grow?

2. Do we have TLs? If not, how will they be identified? If so, do they have the skills to fulfill their role expectations?

3. What are the priorities in my role as a leader?

4. How have we ensured that instructional time is protected from interruptions?

5. What steps should be taken to ensure that my language, decisions, and actions are consistently aligned?

Chapter 2

Crafting and Supporting Strong Missions and Visions

> If you want to build a ship, don't herd people together to collect wood and don't assign them tasks and work, but rather teach them to long for the endless immensity of the sea.
>
> —Antoine de Saint-Exupery

SPOTLIGHT ON EFFECTIVE PRACTICE: A PRINCIPAL MUST HAVE A VISION

At a middle school in a large urban area, teachers reported back to school from summer break to the first pre-school in-service day. The school population comprised approximately 600 students,

(Continued)

(Continued)

30 teachers, an assistant principal, a social worker, and a counselor. On the first day, the principal engaged them in a series of icebreakers that facilitated introductions to each other, and she set the stage for what was expected to be a very productive day.

Fifteen of the 30 teachers had worked at this school for 15 or more years. Ten teachers had tenures of two to five years, and five teachers were new to the profession. After the principal gave an overview of the school, she began sharing the school's history as a community-centered school that was very proud of student achievement during the 1960s and 1970s, when the neighborhood demographics were different. Then the area residents and stakeholders were middle-class blue-collar workers whose primary industry was the steel mills, which were the basis of the local economy for the past two generations.

In addition, she shared her considerable personal family ties to the community. What should have lasted 15 minutes became an hour-long diatribe of the numerous things that were wrong within her community after the steel mills closed in the late 1970s. She described the impact from the influx of families from the Ukraine, South America, and Southeast Asia as being one of the barriers to the school's current achievement gains. She further described the negative results of changes in the school community during her 30-year tenure, 10 of which she had been the principal of this school, citing the shift from a highly upwardly mobile workforce to high unemployment rates and the accompanying increase of the percentage of students receiving free and reduced-priced lunch from 10 to 85 percent as contributing to the school's declining student achievement. Finally, she talked about the 35 percent of students in the school who were achieving at expected levels and the specific strategies that were put in place to assist them.

She gave kudos to those four or five teachers who were responsible for those students' achievement gains while warning the remaining teachers about the hard work that was ahead of them. Finally, teachers were dismissed to prepare their rooms for the opening of school.

On the way to their rooms, several tenured teachers were overheard commenting, "That was the same speech that was given last year, and it still contained no real direction or suggestions for improvement." One teacher said, "If we keep on doing things the same way we have in the past, we are going to get the same results." Not once did the principal share a vision or mission for her school.

Rationale for Visions and Missions

The absence of a vision and mission for a school or school division is a root cause of much dissatisfaction, which can grow like a plague. Everyone has the potential to thrive when directions, expectations, and common understandings are clear. However, when this clarity is absent, the focus and growth are diminished. When visiting schools where visions and missions are not clear or consistently emphasized, a quote paraphrased from Carl Sandburg comes to mind: "We don't know where we're going, but we're on our way."

As we reflect on school leadership, it is helpful to ask several key questions about the value of specifically focusing on achievement and improvements. These questions include but are not limited to the following:

- How can my leadership support a school culture that promotes student improvement?

- What are the most significant factors that are necessary when creating a school culture that supports the academic achievement of all students?

- How important are the teachers' and administrators' roles in in this process?

- Is the support that the school receives from the community sufficient?

- Are the policies created by school boards interpreted in ways that provide equity and accessible opportunities for all students?

The responses to these questions and many others can help shape, strengthen, and sustain school missions. For successful leadership endeavors, the common denominators of purpose that brings all other factors together are the vision and mission that is created for the school and invested in by the stakeholders. Crafting, supporting, and sustaining a strong vision and mission of a school or school system requires dedicated and consistent time.

When we discuss transforming schools through fearless conversations and collaborative communications, in regard to crafting a strong vision and mission, this is a good starting place for 21st-century leaders to initiate improvements. What the school in the vignette needs is leaders who will initiate and support fearless conversations about what the school needs to be instead of what it was in the past. The tone should be inspiring and filled with what we call *hopeful realism.* In other words, while telling the truth, leaders need to ensure that other stakeholders develop and foster a sense of ownership in the journey toward success.

The staff would have benefited from an honest and open conversation about their challenges, and this dialogue could have created opportunities for them to use their experiences and perspectives as bricks on the pathways toward change for success. This would have been the perfect time to communicate to the tenured and especially the new teachers how important it would have been to apply their ideas and enthusiasm to all students and their achievement efforts. This would also have been an opportune time for those teachers who had been successful with the 35 percent of students who achieved at acceptable levels to share the strategies, processes, and ideas that enabled their students to reach their goals. It is extremely important for leaders to develop and strengthen their skills that engage stakeholders in their preferred future of the school or district. In other words, what is our collective vision for this school or district, and what are our means to fulfill this purpose?

Visions and Missions Defined

Throughout the country in many schools and school district offices, the mission and/or vision is displayed in a frame that is usually located near the main entrance of the buildings. However, when administrators, teachers, students, and community stakeholders are asked what the vision and/or mission of their school is, there is often silence or a pregnant pause, followed by what they think or believe constitutes a vision and/or mission for their school or school district.

Often their responses are not aligned with what is written, framed and on display.

It is no secret that the most successful businesses in the world have a singular focus that encompasses a strong vision or mission. We are not suggesting that we run our schools and districts like businesses. However, we would be wise to recognize that successful business practices are generally universal and adaptable as we lead successful schools and districts toward successful changes. One of the pillars of their success is focused marketing campaigns with catchy and memorable slogans such as "Coke Is the Real Thing," "The Pepsi Generation," or "There's no place like home."

Lessons that can be learned from that kind of focus are anchored in the visions and missions of these successful companies and their investment in increasing awareness of that focus. How can we ensure that the vision and mission are communicated to other stakeholders?

Before answering this question think about how clear the vision and the mission are for the school and school division where you are invested. We will return to this question later in this chapter.

Once there is a clear vision and mission for the school or school division, it is important that the entire school community knows it and how everyone is able to contribute and support the vision and mission of the school.

To begin this process, distinguishing the vision from the mission is an important first step. Simply stated the vision is the what, and the mission is the how. The vision is the preferred future that is visualized for a school or school division. It is the starting point for discussions about the school's or school districts' immediate needs and what goals should become a reality. The mission is the way that the vision is accomplished. For example, "The vision of our school/school district is to work closely with all stakeholders to successfully educate all students at all levels." The mission statement may then be "We will consistently provide a safe, nurturing environment with a rigorous curriculum that is respectful of students' learning needs." The specificity of the mission will provide guidance for goal setting and work plans to accomplish the vision.

In essence the vision and mission statement should articulate the beliefs and values and define the school's or district's purpose. They establish the long-term direction that guides every aspect of daily operations. To distinguish between the two, a vision statement expresses reason for existence, whereas a mission statement provides an overview of the plans to realize that vision by identifying the service area, target audience, and values and goals of the organization. In drafting appropriate statements for a school or district, it is helpful to think about the answers to the following questions as guidelines.

> *A vision statement expresses reason for existence, whereas a mission statement provides an overview of the plans to realize that vision by identifying the service area, target audience, and values and goals of the organization.*

Vision

- What are the values or beliefs that inform your work?

- What would be the ultimate hope of accomplishment?

Mission

- How do you plan to work toward this broad vision?

- For whose specific benefit does the school or district exist?

(Angelica, 2015)

Creating Visions and Missions

It is important to know how to begin crafting a vision and mission for your school or school division. One way is to begin to identify the stakeholders and then develop a structure to facilitate a dialogue with various stakeholders. The purpose is to determine what they believe about student achievement and school success and what they are willing to work toward together. This helps to put everyone on the same page.

In a school, for example, the stakeholders include but are not limited to the students, parents, teachers, administrators, counselors, school maintenance personnel, cafeteria workers, local businesses, key community organizations, and resource officers. There should be representation from each of the groups invited to participate in the development of the vision and mission. It is very important to ensure that these representatives are or become competent in communicating with those whom they represent, and leaders should not assume that they have this significant skill.

In the course of developing a strong vision and mission, one of the most important steps is to create forums for open dialogue among all stakeholders to encourage all voices to be heard in a manner that increases the number of ideas that can be generated. One principal developed a protocol that initiated the development of a vision and mission statement. In several group sessions of various stakeholders, he gave each participant a 3×5 index card, and on it he asked them to write in a sentence describing what they believed the vision of the school should be.

They were then divided into small groups of five to six participants and asked to discuss their card contents and to agree on or develop one card to represent the group's thinking. After 20 minutes each group had an opportunity to report to the large group. What emerged were several themes that were repeated by each small group.

Those themes were academic achievement, student behavior, school safety and security, student engagement, communications, and instruction. Each of those themes were recorded on chart paper and placed around the room. The large group was asked to go back into their small groups to discuss and prioritize the themes. They then did a gallery walk and collectively wrote a number from one to five (one being the highest) on each theme.

At the conclusion of this activity, academic achievement and instruction were the highest, school safety and security were second highest, and communication third. The participants were then asked to select one person from each group to be a member of the vision and mission team and, using these three themes, to develop the vision and mission of the school.

Another process used by one of the authors is aligned with the research of several successful problem-solving protocols. The first step in those processes began with soliciting the input of key stakeholders after carefully and critically defining their understandings of what achievement meant and how a successful school should look. Stakeholders were encouraged to clearly define achievement and reflect on their ideal possibilities and dreams. The next step involved was to solidify, condense, confirm, and succinctly combine their ideal school into three or fewer positive statements. The results of using these steps were the birth of a powerful vision and increased buy-in from the stakeholders.

Remain Focused on the Purpose

A primary responsibility of school leaders is to develop a clear vision for accomplishing the school's mission. Often these terms are used interchangeably, although they are markedly different. Leaders who maintain the distinctions between the two concepts are generally able to help other stakeholders focus on the goals, means, and processes needed for achieving highly functioning schools. The vision should be articulated in a manner that defines the actual purpose and anchors the goals for the school. The mission specifies the mechanics of collectively fulfilling that purpose. The vision provides stakeholders with aligned understanding of what is important, and the mission provides insights and guidance on how they will remain focused on that understanding. Some may say the vision provides direction to an agreed-upon destination, and the mission provides the specifics of the journey.

The mission statement answers these questions: Why do we exist? and What is our core purpose? The characteristics of a mission statement are that it is short, memorable, and inspiring. A good mission statement should be "market" focused. The market focus is directed to the people we serve and what value we are providing as an organization, and it should reflect what we want to be remembered for. A great example is "To organize the world's information and make it universally accessible and useful" (Google).

> *The mission statement answers these questions: Why do we exist? and What is our core purpose? The characteristics of a mission statement are that it is short, memorable, and inspiring.*

The how to involves first and foremost people. Although it may be impossible to get all of the people in your school or district involved all at once, surveys can be administered that will allow all stakeholders to share their core beliefs.

Information is another essential need. Previous mission statements and the current mission statement may be starting points. Ensuring that stakeholders know the contents of the mission and vision regardless of whether they were a part of its development is crucial.

Finally, a planning process is a necessary tool to complete the development of the mission (OnStrategy, n.d.). Using an existing process or creating one that incorporates unique needs is fine as each involves getting stakeholders together to create a visual of all perspectives, interests, and understandings. This investment creates stronger support and buy-in for the work that needs to be done.

SPOTLIGHT ON EFFECTIVE PRACTICE: MAKING IT WORK

One newly hired middle school principal found an effective means to developing a clearer vision and mission statement at a school that was already filled with traditions, customs, and expectations that were not aligned with current students or community needs and expectations. She first ensured that stakeholders had a sense of ownership and voice in the review and revision of the vision and updating the mission by identifying the representatives from various populations of the school. Faculty, partners, students, and parent representatives collaborated to develop the new vision and mission, and each department within the school shared its commitment to focusing on the mission by clarifying its strategies and work plans to accomplish the aligned understanding.

Everyone was required to articulate how the functions, activities, requests, promotions, and practices within classrooms and the school's culture were a part of the vision and the mission. To address the vision of the school, "The Academic Achievement of all Students," certain agreed-upon schoolwide classroom practices were implemented. They included the following:

Practices to Ensure the Academic Achievement of All Students

- All teachers had to first greet students at the door at the beginning of the class period.

- They had to have a do-now assignment on the chalkboard when students entered the classroom to immediately engage them in the lesson they were about to learn, to help the teacher to have an understanding of their prior knowledge, or to help the teacher introduce new material.

- All teachers were required to have one or more instructional activities that actively engaged students in small groups, large groups, or independent study.

- All teachers were also required to have an exit ticket for students before they left the classroom to know what was taught was learned.

- When completing a field trip request, an explanation was required to ensure that the trip would support or further the goals toward the mission and vision; in the absence of such an explanation, the field trip was denied.

- All field trips also had to connect to standards of learning objectives, and the teachers had to develop assessments or projects that were related to these standards.

- Teachers were required to keep data on the achievement levels of students based on those out-of-school experiences mainly through projects or service learning experiences.

Ongoing data collection on the progress of the strategies to fulfill the mission provided essential feedback to school leaders. Establishing benchmarks on a timeline helped everyone monitor the growth and changes and provided essential opportunities to make adjustments to ensure success. This monitoring also had the benefits of helping maintain everyone's attention to the goals or refocused people's efforts when needed.

If the principal in the "A Principal Must Have a Vision" vignette had presented achievement data, by subject, by grade level, by ethnicity and socioeconomic level, her teachers would have had a succinct perspective of where areas of improvement were needed for remediation and enrichment activities. The data would have painted a clearer picture for grade-level and subject-specific communication around the types of curriculum, instructional activities, and planning activities that would have been needed to ensure stronger academic achievement for all students.

Using Data to Manage

Fearless leaders in the 21st century know or learn when to seize the moment to have rich discussions about data that generate thinking around common goals and supports teachers in their efforts to infuse their creativity and innovative ideas to address these areas of concern. Additionally, a fearless leader in this age of accountability would collect data teacher by teacher in each subject area, looking for those teachers who have consistently high rates of failure, and begin to craft some necessary and courageous conversations that should occur to help them become more successful.

Leaders often struggle over what data should be collected, how often it should be collected, and how to use it to make instructional and other decisions that are aligned to the vision and mission of the school or school division. It is our belief that the vision and mission of the school should be revisited each year, and benchmarks for intermittent review should be established using current data. In addition to the typical standardized data that are often available, soft data that should be considered include, but are not limited to, graduation rates, achievement data, attendance data (student and staff), parental contact, and community participation in school activities.

According to the Task Force on Research in Educational Research, "effective educational leaders help their schools to develop or endorse visions that embody the best thinking about teaching and learning. School leaders inspire others to reach for ambitious goals" (Gabriel & Farmer, 2009, p. 3). The ability of school leaders to bring people together to work toward a meaningful common goal is imperative in the creation of strong vision and mission statements. The school leader who encourages group thinking as opposed to individual ideas will create a broader platform for collaboration and collegiality.

As mentioned earlier, crafting and accomplishing a strong vision and mission requires dedicated time, focus, and energy from the stakeholders. The next step is that all members of the initiating and creating groups or committees need to communicate with the constituents they represent to discuss the results of their work, prioritize issues, and solicit reactions responses and feedback. Leaders need to ensure that this critical step occurs as these communications are essential to the sense of ownership and understandings that will be needed from everyone involved. Many years ago, the former executive director of the National Association of Secondary School Principals, Dr. Gerald Tarrozi (2003), captured the importance of this inclusive step by stating, "If the principal of the school is the only one who creates the vision and mission of the school, it is an illusion."

Once feedback is received from each group of stakeholders, it will then be the responsibility of the core group of leaders to facilitate additional discussions, review the priorities of their initial work, and develop a draft of the vision and mission statement to present to all stakeholders for further input or approval. When the approved vision and mission statements are determined, a useful strategy to fine-tune is called the *elevator speech*. An elevator speech can be defined by one's ability to articulate the vision and mission of a school to one or more individuals who boards an elevator on the first floor before it arrives at the 20th floor. The ability of all leaders in the school or division to give an elevator speech sends a powerful message to the school community and its stakeholders

The ability of all leaders in the school or division to give an elevator speech sends a powerful message to the school community and its stakeholders because it demonstrates a singular purpose and tells in a succinct manner how it will be done—with one voice.

because it demonstrates a singular purpose geared toward those values and beliefs that inform the work and tells in a succinct manner how it will be done—with *one voice.*

Unify Stakeholders

A good example of an entire school division having one voice was how this occurred during the tenure of Dr. Deborah Jewell Sherman, former superintendent of Richmond City Public School (2002–2008). She developed consensus among stakeholders and articulated one vision for the school division: "The Academic Achievement of **ALL** Students. Failure is not an option!" (Richmond City Public Schools, n.d.). To her credit, employees, students, and parents knew, understood, and could recite the vision of the school division. During the six years of her leadership, a failing school district evolved into one of the most successful school districts academically across the state. In 2002, more than 95 percent of the 53 schools in the school division had not achieved state accreditation, and by 2008, more than 98 percent of all schools in Richmond City achieved or exceeded the state accreditation requirements that began with one voice.

Having one voice or a clearly understood vision in a school division sends a powerful message to the community that it serves. Communicating this message to our communities is equally as important regarding the priorities. The focus and emphasis of our work are those things cited in our mission statement. It is equally important that a strong mission includes component parts and determine how to measure its success. The mission of most schools and school divisions is to create a nurturing learning environment that prepares students to solve problems creatively, use resources advantageously, and work cooperatively with others to meet the challenges of being college and career ready and to enter the workforce with 21st-century skills.

Leaders and stakeholders should collaboratively define what a nurturing learning environment is and how it should look, sound, and feel. The definition of nurturing is to support and encourage others to grow, develop, and succeed. For example, when walking through a school that has a nurturing environment, it should feature visible evidence that all students are given the social, emotional, and psychological support that will provide them best access to completion of the mission. The evidence may include but not be limited to observing behaviors and conversations that clearly indicate students and adults have mutual respect for each other; observing teachers encouraging, motivating, engaging, and rewarding students in appropriate ways; and observing evidence of support systems in place that facilitate students' social and emotional needs.

SPOTLIGHT ON EFFECTIVE PRACTICE: STRATEGIES THAT SUPPORT THE VISION AND MISSION

A high school principal was meeting with his leadership team during their regularly scheduled Monday morning meeting. During the previous weekend a fight had occurred at a house party that was attended by his students. All information suggested that the conflict that originated at the party would find its way into the school Monday morning. This is not an uncommon occurrence in any school community where there are conflicts within family groups, between gangs, and among other factions within the different neighborhoods. Disputes that have nothing to do with the school are frequently brought to school for resolution, management, or other amelioration.

(Continued)

(Continued)

One of the primary responsibilities of all teachers in this school was to look, listen, and be alert and visible between all class changes and to act proactively in reducing potential problems. Teachers received seminars, workshops, and other learning sessions from police, security personnel, and other experts to learn about warning signs and look-fors regarding potential conflicts.

In addition, earlier that year the principal and his leadership team developed a schoolwide teacher-student mentorship and advisory program. Every adult in the building including support staff were assigned to work with a group of a minimum of 12 students. These groups evolved into small family-like units, and the master schedule was redesigned to allow these groups to meet biweekly for 30 minutes during the school day. During these meetings lesson plans anchored in several themes were distributed. These plans were developed by a group of teachers representing the various disciplines.

For the first three meetings that year, the theme was conflict resolution. Students were provided with scenarios illustrating different types of conflicts, and during the first two meetings, students and teachers discussed and role-played ways in which to resolve conflict that come into the school, to mediate those conflicts between individuals, to help students make better choices and decisions, and to learn how actions can escalate into violent encounters. To support this mentoring unit, the principal and one of his assistant principals broadcast on the school's closed circuit television station a simulation of a fight between them and then the steps in the mediation process that should follow. Not only did the students think that this was "cool," but they also began to immediately practice those skills demonstrated by the administrators during the broadcast and those skills discussed and practiced in their meetings.

On this Monday morning, no one knew how effective the lessons were until the five combatants from the weekend's conflict entered the building and went directly to their mentors and asked for a mediation among them. There was a level of trust that had been developed between the adults and students in these biweekly meetings that created a nurturing and trusting environment where students would rather do the right thing to maintain a peaceful and safe school than fight to make a point and then be suspended or face expulsion for disrupting the school environment.

Through these and other teacher–student mentor experiences, other themes were developed. For example, when a popular student was killed in an automobile accident, most students had never experienced the death of someone close to them. One of the lesson plans that was developed was titled Death and Dying and the Grieving Process. The school brought in trained professional counselors to meet with students and teachers in their mentor groups and provide an opportunity to not only grieve for their lost friend but also to create a forum to deepen understandings that adults cared enough about them to make this a priority over the day's lessons. During the following days, students were still very sad but were able to support each other through the grieving process, honoring the memory of the deceased in positive ways and celebrating her life.

The principal believed that to fully achieve stated nurturing goals in the mission of this school, it would be beneficial for all students to complete a service learning project. As a graduation requirement all students had to spend at least 10 hours a year completing a service learning project. They had a choice to work independently, in pairs or small groups, to contribute positively to the lives of others. During their senior year they had to present their projects at a service learning fair held at the end of the year, just prior to graduation. Students completed these projects by working in animal shelters, working with the elderly in nursing homes, and taking on environmental projects.

(Continued)

(Continued)

One of the projects that received statewide acclaim was done by a group of students who decided to clean up a five-mile stretch of polluted river. This particular project began with eight students, but once it got started, participation increased to about 15 students. The students developed detailed plans to determine how to safely remove abandoned car parts, old tires, refrigerators, plumbing parts, and other debris from the water and how to discard these things properly. They spent the entire fall and spring completing this project, and what was once a much-polluted, five-mile eyesore stretch of water became restored to a pristine look similar to when Lewis and Clark lived and traveled this waterway. The collaboration, cooperation, and dedication to this project were outstanding.

Although students were required to complete only 10 hours of service each year for a total of 40 hours over a four-year period, there was not a single project that students didn't spend a minimum of 100 hours completing. Even after graduation, many of the students still volunteered at the animal shelter and nursing homes. Many of the students who were involved in the local river project went on to study environmental science in college.

Another example of what can help leaders maintain the vision and mission of the school or district is that when teachers or administrators make requests to attend conferences, they should be required to ensure that the conference and the concurrent sessions within it are aligned to the vision and mission of the school or district. In addition, upon their return from the conference, they should be required to share and convey their learnings and understandings gleaned from the conference with other stakeholders.

One of the authors facilitated meetings with conference attendees to ensure that all were prepared to fulfill the expectations from their attendance and defined their accountability. The planning meeting helped ensure that everyone had the tools to capture the essential elements of sessions and that everyone knew in advance who would be attending agreed-upon sessions. Note-taking strategies, reporting, presenting protocols, and article-writing options were discussed. Attendees were able to choose the method-ologies for sharing and reteaching their colleagues that were com-patible with their skills. A calendar was developed that informed everyone when the sharing would happen and in what format the sharing would occur.

Summary

The contents of this chapter examine some of the unresolved challenges that educators experience in aligning curriculum with standards and provide some specific and doable solutions to those challenges. The chapter also articulates the power of effective feedback to effect change. Many appraisal systems have more to do with preserving jobs and fulfilling regulations than bringing about change in today's classrooms. Without accurate, honest, supportive, and specific feedback, another opportunity for growth and positive change is missed. To craft and conquer strong missions and visions in school is to ensure that everyone has a voice in the process of developing, implementing, and evaluating the mission and vision of the school and how effective feedback comes from all stakeholders in the school community.

Setting specific achievement goals as a part of building the mission for the school is a challenging endeavor. If it is done well, the process will involve stakeholders who all have their own ideas and priorities, which may not completely match or align. Still, it is critical to identify the most important goals for the school and to focus on ways to move the school forward most effectively. What is often neglected or tacked on as an afterthought are the processes and protocols that should be employed to create a vision and mission that are aligned.

If the mission statement includes an emphasis on a nurturing environment, then stakeholders must be clear on what that means. For students to become college and career ready, and to enter the workforce with 21st-century skills, it is important that practices within the school division reflect this clarity. The types of activities that occur in teacher–student mentor programs through the use of thematic units, developed by teachers and students, give students an opportunity to develop additional good communication skills. It also gives them the ability to work successfully with others to solve complex problems, and it provides opportunities to develop the ability to use a variety of resources to work toward common goals.

In creating a vision and mission for a school or school district, there must be a curriculum that provides the experiences and insights that will define the desired future options for all students (vision) and have a well-thought-out plan as to how to get them there (mission). When developing either a vision or a mission statement, it is critical to ensure that it is aligned to the curriculum that is offered to students. When preparing your student to utilize 21st-century skills to enter the workplace, course offerings should be designed to accomplish this task. Keeping in mind that all students will not be college bound, it is necessary to have a well-rounded curriculum to prepare some students to attend a technical development school or to enter a community college to explore career possibilities, participate in intern programs that will train them in technical fields, or prepare them to enter the military.

Too often leaders' understanding or knowledge base about various curriculums offered in schools or within the school divisions are limited to what they once taught. Frequently, there is insufficient time, access to, or interest in extending their familiarity with entire school offerings at the secondary level. Although it is not necessary to have intimate knowledge of each subject, it is, however, essential to have a working knowledge of the goals of each course and to have a strong knowledge base of exemplary teaching practices. It is difficult to lead others in directions where one has little or no knowledge or experience. It is even more difficult to lead stakeholders when destinations and directions for arriving are unclear or absent. To fulfill the agreed-upon vision and mission, instructional leadership is critical. The most effective means of accomplishing this is through developing and strengthening the ability to lead, guide, and support faculties through providing effective, fair, and accurate feedback.

Reflections

The following questions are designed to provoke additional thinking and discussions about crafting and supporting strong missions and visions.

1. How are the current vision and mission of our school aligned with the objectives and goals of our school and/or district?

2. What steps are needed to strengthen the vision and mission in our school and/or district?

3. What is the elevator speech of my school and/or district? (If you don't have one, what should it be?)

4. What evidence exists that the stakeholders know and support the mission and vision of the school and/or district?

Chapter 3

Improving Through Effective Feedback

> Make feedback normal. Not a performance review.
>
> —Ed Batista

> We all need people who will give us feedback. That's how we improve.
>
> —Bill Gates

Feedback Is Critical

There are certain nonnegotiable practices that should be paramount for all school leaders. One of these is ensuring that there are ongoing and monitored processes and benchmarks in place to keep everyone informed of the progress toward achieving the vision and agreed-upon mission. This requires benchmark observances, progress measurement, and sharing this information with stakeholders. Sharing this data in a formative way is critical to improving and making adjustments during the journey and, thus, maximizing the opportunities for success. This chapter discusses ways to monitor and provide feedback that leaders need to facilitate to remain focused upon accomplishing the vision and mission.

Anchoring Improvements in Data

Although it is widely accepted and known that data collecting and usage are crucial to school improvement, there continues to be much discussion about what data to collect and debates on how to use them to set goals and make decisions. Though standardized data are commonly accessed and used, it is also important to consider the information that can be harvested from other sources. For example, collecting and sharing information from schoolwide walkthroughs, clinical rounds, or learning walk systems and sharing data collected from classroom and other work-space observations can help deepen our understandings on elements of a school's culture that need to be addressed. In addition, creating transparent opportunities for student and parental feedback to leaders and sharing that feedback with teachers in nonevaluative ways can also be highly beneficial to processes designed to improve student achievement. The keys here are transparency and sharing.

Developing school-level and student-level data collection processes provides more opportunities for stakeholders' involvement and can yield more comprehensive and sustainable results. The labor intensity of this process is front-loaded and can be prohibitive to many who are seeking quicker results. However, the level at which the individual school collects and analyzes data is critical for high levels of achievement. The following model (see Table 3.1) was adapted from one used in Richmond City Public Schools, Richmond, Virginia, in kindergarten through Grade 12 from 2002 through 2008, and the results were astonishing, as noted in Chapter 2.

DATA COLLECTION SHEET

Teacher: _____ Subject: _____ Period: _____

Essential Skill(s)/Standards Observed: _____

On Target with Pacing Guide (Check One): Yes _____ No _____

Table 3.1

In-Classroom Intervention Strategies	Out-of-Classroom Intervention Strategies
In-Classroom Intervention Strategies	Out-of-Classroom Intervention Strategies
In-Classroom Enrichment Strategies	Out-of-Classroom Enrichment Strategies

Source: Adapted from Richmond City Public School model.

The power of this model is that at each level, teachers must give some thought to providing intervention or enrichment experiences designed to improve or advance student achievement. The adaptability of this model (see Table 3.2) for leaders is it is a user-friendly

DATA COLLECTION SHEET

Teacher: ___Mrs. Jones___ Subject: ___English 9___ Period: ___3rd___

Essential Skill(s)/Standards Observed: ___Analyzing Figurative Language___

On Target with Pacing Guide (Check One): Yes _X_ No __ Date _Today_

Table 3.2. Sample Completed Form

In-Classroom Intervention Strategies	Out-of-Classroom Intervention Strategies
Making inferences using selected text	After-school peer tutoring program
Drawing Conclusions	
In-Classroom Intervention Strategies	Out-of-Classroom Intervention Strategies
Visualizing	After-school homework support program
Comparing and contrasting	Partnership with local church to tutor
In-Classroom Enrichment Strategies	Out-of-Classroom Enrichment Strategies
Write a story using figurative language	Saturday school intervention for remediation and enrichment

Source: Adapted from Richmond City Public School model.

way for leaders to collect information to improve instruction and examine the school's culture and base it on standards upon which teachers are evaluated. Thus, evaluation standards become a more useful tool to help teachers improve. A revised form could be the example in Table 3.3.

Setting specific achievement goals, for many school leaders, is often challenging on multiple levels. However, it is very important to identify common focus areas within contents that when

DATA COLLECTION SHEET

Teacher: _____ Subject: _____ Period: _____

Essential Skill(s)/Standards Observed: _____

On Target with School Improvement Goals): Yes _____ No _____

Table 3.3. Goal Setting to Focus Improvements

Contribution to Department/ Grade-Level Goals	Schoolwide/Grade-Level Goals
Contribution to Department/ Grade-Level Goals	Schoolwide/Grade-Level Goals
Contribution to Department/ Grade-Level Goals	Schoolwide/Grade-Level Goals

Source: Adapted from Richmond City Public School model.

improved, will move the school toward accomplishing its mission most effectively. Even more important, leaders must ensure that teachers have input in identifying specific achievement goals for individuals and groups of students by holding regular data examination meetings. In addition, it is also wise to take advantage of information learned during parent–teacher

DATA COLLECTION SHEET

Teacher: ___Mrs. Jones___ Subject: ___English___ Period: _3rd_

Essential Skill(s)/Standards Observed: _Analyzing Figurative Language_

On Target with Pacing Guide (Check One): Yes _X_ No __ Date _Today_

Table 3.4. Sample Completed Form

Contribution to Department/ Grade-Level Goals	Schoolwide/Grade-Level Goals
Develop skills for students who will learn to understand and appreciate imaginative literature	Exposing students to a variety of literary genres
Contribution to Department/ Grade-Level Goals	**Schoolwide/Grade-Level Goals**
Examining how figurative language occurs in everyday language	Improving students' communication skills
Contribution to Department/ Grade-Level Goals	**Schoolwide/Grade-Level Goals**
Making inferences, drawing conclusions, visualizing, and comparing and contrasting	Improving students' literacy skills

Source: Adapted from Richmond City Public School model.

conference days (among other nontraditional and underutilized sources) to maximize plans for improvements academically and socially (see the Sample Completed Form in Table 3.4).

Setting goals and providing feedback to students is a means of guiding and helping them think about and strengthen their own learning. Along those same lines, setting goals and providing meaningful and consistent feedback to teachers can be one of the most powerful practices that a school

Setting goals and providing meaningful and consistent feedback to teachers can be one of the most powerful practices that a school leader can do to enhance professional growth and improve student achievement.

leader can do to enhance professional growth and improve student achievement. Goal setting based upon student achievement data helps target instruction in ways to specifically address greater learning needs. Various forms of feedback should be provided for the improvement of classroom practices and schoolwide growth as well as actually using existing feedback from several types of assessments. Here is another powerful input opportunity from teacher leaders (TLs).

Goal Setting to Focus Improvements

The words *goal setting* are frequently used as a reference to something people need to do, want to do, or intend to do some time in the future. Using these words so frequently often diminishes their real importance, when in fact, these are not simply words but rather a serious intention. A goal is actually a visualized target that should activate people who may be thinking of completing a specific task. This visualization also acts as a stimulant and motivator to achieve the goal (Egan, n.d.) Goals are essential steps in any improvement process, but often they are not measured to determine how successful the work toward achieving them is. They define how leaders can proceed to fulfill the mission.

Improvements require measuring the impact of the efforts to achieve goals through evaluations and assessments. Educators often inappropriately interchange the concepts of evaluations, assessments, and feedback. Evaluations and assessments are generally about making a decision or judgment about the value of something. In contrast, feedback is generally about providing focused and timely information that allows for reflections about improvements. Just as feedback provide students with guidance and help them think about their own learning, providing nonevaluative feedback to teachers can be one of the most powerful practices that a school leader can do to enhance professional growth and impact student achievement. Various forms of feedback to teachers could be provided to enhance instructional improvements, schoolwide growth, and using data from assessments. One of the more popularly successful options today is coaching.

In some districts, professional development committees meet with administrators to establish professional goals for all teachers within the district. Many goals such as literacy and technology are interdisciplinary. For example, raising standardized reading test scores might be a district goal that requires support across grade levels and content areas. The professional development committee might provide seminars, workshops, and access to resources to provide all teachers help with improving their students' literacy skills. However, according to researchers, much of what we know about good support involves helping teachers help themselves. This includes establishing and supporting processes and/or programs that will provide them with nonevaluative feedback to help them enhance, strengthen, and enrich existing skills. Strategies that incorporate this type of useful feedback are often absent from the repertoire of support. In addition to what the district initiates, some school goals may focus on literacy improvement in specific subject areas by providing certain content teachers with opportunities to align their curricula with state standards that include literacy expectations.

Providing Targeted Feedback

It is very important for school leaders to know the difference between feedback and commentary. Feedback can be defined as information about reactions to a person's performance of a task that is used as a basis for improvement. Commentary can be defined as an expression of opinions or offerings of explanations about an event or situation. The terms are often used interchangeably and often inappropriately.

Let's look at coaches and music teachers. A successful track, football, or tennis coach gives accurate feedback to improve an athlete's speed, agility, and muscle memory by emphasizing the mechanics involved in physically performing on the field or court and, thus, allowing the athlete to make adjustments in his or her ongoing practice to accomplish game goals and reduce injuries. This is also true with successful music teachers who provide accurate feedback individually and collectively on the overall synchronization of the instruments or voices to come together in a melodic harmony.

John Hattie (2009) after decades of research, revealed that feedback was among the most powerful influences on achievement and acknowledged that he has "struggled to understand the concept" (p.173). Grant Wiggins (2012) cites seven keys to effective feedback. They are goal referenced, tangible and transparent, actionable, user-friendly, timely, ongoing, and consistent. When looking at the overall effect of feedback, it also should provide a forum for discussion and reflection on the part of the observer and observee.

Moreover, it is important to be honest and straightforward in giving negative feedback. Often negative feedback is buried in a conversation about what worked as opposed to what didn't work to improve the achievement of students. For school leaders it is often easier to give positive feedback because it makes teachers feel good. But as school leaders

> *It is important to be honest and straightforward in giving negative feedback. As school leaders we have a responsibility to ensure that teachers are accountable for what happens in their classrooms and the outcomes that are the result of good instruction.*

we have a responsibility to ensure that teachers are accountable for what happens in their classrooms and the outcomes that are the result of good instruction. School leaders must have courageous and fearless conversations when necessary in the feedback process.

It is unfortunate, but many experienced and novice leaders determine that nonevaluative strategies such as walk-throughs, instructional-clinical rounds, and learning walks are too time-consuming and, thus, are reluctant to invest the necessary time to use these strategies. In reality, our experiences have taught us that the investment of the necessary time in using these strategies are well worth it as the payoff results in improved instruction and improved student learning.

Essential to providing growth feedback to teachers is the need to overcome certain political barriers that can "taint" this process. Some leaders experience barriers and negative reactions from union representatives, teachers who are underperforming, and colleagues who fear that these leaders will create more work for them to do when they already have enough on their plates.

These barriers are realistic and require a courageous focus, good timing, and creative strategies if positive changes are to occur. For example, choosing which teachers to begin the process with is important; choosing the right time to deliver feedback and choosing the best format in which to deliver the feedback must be pre-planned. In addition, the feedback must be perceived as a genuine effort to help rather than as punitive or ego boosting.

The lack of useful feedback prohibits communications and collaboration—both much needed elements in successful schools. Collaboration in a learning environment is required if honesty, openness, sharing, and growth are priorities. For example, collaboration among educators is essential as it pertains to analyzing student achievement. The us-versus-them mentality that is present in many schools between administrators and teachers interferes with or sometimes limits meaningful analysis. Again, using strategies such as clinical rounds and learning walks help build collegiality and trust that facilitate changes, growth, and improvements.

This analysis can inform curriculum development and help further develop the school's feedback processes for students and teachers. To encourage teacher collaboration with regard to curriculum and assessment, the processes for teachers' growth and improvements should be separate from their evaluations and be included in over-all school operations to allow for stronger and more proactive shifting toward or integration of this type of site-based support.

Informal and formal assessment systems should include provisions that allow administrators or teacher leaders to provide feedback to colleagues based on specific principles that are anchored in the foundations of solid instruction. Because sound instruction is what drives schoolwide improvement, providing all teachers with feed-back based on the same research on instructional design and deliv-ery criteria can help ensure that what is happening in schools is of the highest quality and pushes schools toward greater excellence.

The consistency of these types of systems can be used to provide feedback in useful increments of time based on specific knowledge and skills that can help improve teacher practice and thus stu-dent achievement. An example is if the decision by instructional leaders is anchored in the research on how students learn best, it is usually wiser if the consensual agreements can focus on instruc-tional design using the work of one set of learning styles research or on one multiple intelligences set of research rather than on both learning styles and multiple intelligences.

Using a focused feedback and practice model, teachers can more easily embrace opportunities to receive growth feedback from the administrators, instructional coaches, or TLs when positive relationships are employed as a part of the school's culture. Most teachers want to increase their pedagogical skills regarding the strategies and behaviors of identifying and focusing on certain areas of strengths and weaknesses. However, there are often unclear collaborative agreements on how this is to be done.

Developing a process for consistent feedback can be powerful support and intervention that help address the creating and sustaining of a viable work environment and achieving the school's mission, as mentioned in the previous two chapters. The implementation of regular feedback cycles could serve as engaging benchmark sessions that build knowledge and provide incremental feedback for teachers' growth that is separate from their evaluations. It is similar to the concept of asking them to provide formative feedback to students for the purpose of ongoing learning. Engaging in a process of continued refinement and improvement of professional practices and the processes and strategies used in the classroom will undoubtedly improve student achievement.

This is another of the reasons that consistent and focused walk-throughs, clinical or instructional rounds, and learning walks are strongly recommended. Ongoing feedback is vitally important as well-designed protocols can provide nonjudgmental and consistent feedback that is designed to promote growth. Again, this is true for faculty, staff, and students. Although there are several walk-through protocols, we favor City, Elmore, Fiarman, and Teitel's (2009) clinical rounds, which require several steps: The observers should clearly articulate their goals and problem of practice prior to the event; visit the observee; collaboratively debrief, reflecting on what was learned during the session; and then plan the next level of work using the new data. Whether using the instructional rounds protocols in small groups or as individuals, the focus remains on obtaining information for learning and improvement.

Learning walks are another cost-effective protocol that is very effective in providing nonthreatening and useful feedback. Learning walks are a transparent process that involves multiple stakeholders who seek useful information on agreed-upon targets for school or district improvements; the building management and operations, alignment of instruction, or aspects of the school's culture. Post walks involve opportunities to explore possible solutions to challenges, clarify next steps toward improvements, identify support that is needed, and develop ways to monitor and assess progress. These walks are usually anchored in some concern identified in school data, and the participants clarify the specifics prior to beginning the activity. They are empowering to stakeholders and are highly recommended to strengthen and develop leadership among staff, parents, and even students.

Several school divisions around the country are utilizing learning walks to focus on what students are learning, students' interactions with the teachers and with their peers, and the levels of students' overall engagement in what is being taught. An effective learning walks strategy, also known as a type of instructional rounds, begin with discussions about what it is that students should know and be able to do. Before each walk, the facilitator makes the focus clear. Each walker is asked to observe the presence of and to consider the effectiveness of the three Rs: rigor, relevance, and relationships. During the classroom visits, they observe the level of rigor, the relevance of the content or skills being taught, and the quality of the relationships the teacher has with the students and the students have with each other (Guild, 2012). This can result in high-quality feedback to multiple stakeholders.

Albemarle County Virginia describes their learning walk model as a reflective practice that guides classroom visits. They define what a learning walk is, when they should occur, and when to conduct them. They have a strong focus on the curriculum implementation, the actual lesson being taught, and the quality of students' engagement. This model incorporates a time for a reflective dialogue with open-ended, nonjudgmental, reflective conversations that may occur at the individual teacher level or at the professional learning community level, generating powerful and practical feedback to stakeholders (Albemarle County Public Schools, n.d.).

Albemarle County protocol is anchored in the work of Schlechty (2011), who sees the primary work of teachers as developing tasks and experiences that engage students in learning significant content, processes, and skills. He believes that teachers can do this by attending to the design qualities of context and the design qualities of choice. These elements are consistent with the teacher performance appraisal rubrics and the framework for quality learning and directly connect to and align with components of the professional learning community model and the division's strategic plan. Additionally, Schlechty's "engaging qualities" are incorporated into this learning walks model.

In addition, walkers use the engaging qualities along with other data collected (including one-on-one mini-interviews with students) to indicate whether the classroom is engaged. This is typically the case if three or more engaging qualities are present or students are on task (students are doing what is asked of them, but fewer than three engaging qualities are present) or off task (students are generally not doing what is being asked of them).

Rigor, relevance, and student engagement are the cornerstones of work done by the International Center for Leadership in Education. Upon their inception in 1993 by Bill Daggett (2015), these criteria set the stage for what is succinctly necessary to be observed and have a direct link to what creates highly effective learning environments and, at the same time, provides effective feedback to teachers.

Another process that provides useful feedback to teachers is the protocols promoted by the International Center for Leadership in Education, including the collaborative instructional review. In this review teachers preplan what they want the reviewer to look for and meet with him or her to discuss it. Together they can decide if rigor, relevance, or student engagement needs to be the focus of the upcoming observation. They can choose, one, two, or all three. Reviewers use this tool to provide the teachers with valuable, nonevaluative feedback. Whether a walk-through or a full review is conducted, afterward the teachers meet with the reviewer(s) to have a collaborative discussion about what was observed. Afterward, there is time allotted for reflection by the teacher and reviewer(s). It is important to note that this tool can be used with one or more reviewers, and they have the ability to calibrate their responses and share them with the teacher.

This is a powerful tool for use with new leaders and leaders who desire to enrich their feedback-providing skills as it has a high degree of interrater reliability when used with fidelity. Leaders play key roles throughout this initiative by coaching and facilitating each step of the process. The power in this type of walk-through is that the focus is again on the learning of the observer rather than the teacher observed. To establish this practice within a school, it is recommended to begin with department chairs, team leaders, and instructional coaches as a powerful and practical way to enhance through modeling, their observational and feedback skills.

Coaching for Growth

The growth of the observer is the focus of any walk-though process. This protocol also strengthens and promotes the building of additional leadership skills. It can be led by teacher leaders, administrators, coaches, and other stakeholders. The process promotes and gives concrete support toward the shared school vision as it is in action and provides teachers compelling opportunities to learn from each other and reflect upon their own practices. Follow-up discussions during departmental or team meetings can expand the growth options for all participants. A huge benefit of this protocol is the continued growth and improvements that ultimately translate to improved learning opportunities for students. It is *free* and helps educator stakeholders help themselves.

SPOTLIGHT ON EFFECTIVE PRACTICE: BEFORE THE WALK-THROUGH OR OBSERVATION

A principal for 16 years had a habit of visiting as many classrooms as possible each day. Teachers and students were used to these visits, and their frequency and consistency caused minimal disruptions. He followed the 80/20 protocol, which meant that as an instructional leader, he and his administrative team, on a daily basis, were expected to spend 80 percent of their time in classrooms and 20 percent of their time completing managerial tasks.

(Continued)

(Continued)

To facilitate the practicalities of this protocol, the assistant principals and support staff were informed that the principal would be in classrooms and, other than an emergency, should not be disturbed. A formal schedule was developed on a weekly basis to allow for each administrator to adhere to this practice. When three administrators were in classrooms, there was always one available to deal with disciplinary and other issues. A diplomatic discussion was held with the superintendent to ensure his awareness of this practice, and he supported the focus on instruction. It didn't eliminate his calls during the day, but he did not pull the principal out of classrooms unless it was an emergency. Often he would simply leave a message for the call to be returned later.

The next group he communicated this practice to was the parents. To accommodate this instructional focus, meetings with them occurred early in the morning before the first bell or late in the afternoon after the last bell. In the monthly newsletter and at parent–teacher organization meetings, parents and the community were reminded of the primary school goal of implementing high-quality instruction and that the school's leadership would remain focused on this goal through consistent classroom visitations; the majority of his parents and community members were very supportive of the 80/20 process. A few people mentioned concerns about principal availability, but those concerns were mitigated when the standardized test scores made exponential gains each year.

SPOTLIGHT ON EFFECTIVE PRACTICE: THE WALK-THROUGH

The walk-through is a method of getting a snapshot of what learning is taking place in a classroom. A walk-through can take as little time as five minutes or less per classroom visit but usually not more than 20 minutes, depending upon the size of the desired snapshot. Generally, each day, walk-through routes were planned for the following day. It took about two months before teachers became accustomed to the principal, assistant principals, and TLs visiting their rooms on a daily basis. However, once they determined that the visits weren't a "got-ya" exercise on the part of administrative team, they became receptive to the feedback that was given them after the visits.

When the principal was shadowed for a few days, the observer noticed that time was not spent equally in each classroom. Some classrooms were visited on consecutive days, whereas others were visited intermittently. The reasons for this differentiation varied from seeing how well a teacher began his or her lesson to how a teacher may have made transitions between activities or simply seeing the level of student engagement from day to day and lesson to lesson. The point was also made during the planning process throughout the year, to see various teachers at different times of the day.

We recommend clarity about the look-fors during walk-throughs and believe that it would be best to start with observing what students are doing more than what teachers are doing. When walking into a classroom, observers can know immediately if the classroom

> *We recommend clarity about the look-fors during walk-throughs and believe that it would be best to start with observing what students are doing more than what teachers are doing.*

is student centered or teacher centered by the work students are doing, whether they are working independently or in small groups, and whether there is visible evidence of student work around the room.

It is also very important to listen to the language that the teacher uses. For example, are the teachers asking low-level comprehension and recall questions, like how, what, and why? Or is the teacher

(Continued)

(Continued)

using higher-order thinking questions that ask students to compare and contrast, evaluate, list, synthesize, judge, justify, or create. And most important, can one hear students using the same higher-order thinking language as they work in small groups completing projects or solving problems? The focus should remain on student learning rather than teachers teaching.

As principals, one of our practices while doing walk-through visits was taking copious notes on what was observed in terms of the rigor and relevance of lessons and the level of student engagement during the snapshot visits. Many teachers appreciated receiving sticky notes or e-mails about something that was observed during the visits. Notes were easy to place on the teachers' desks before leaving the room. If there were questions about something observed, it was a simple matter to include a request for clarification.

Genuine and factually based praise went a long way when it was consistent. It is also a way to remind teachers that they are valued and respected for what they do every day. It helps leaders to take them further along the continuum of success for themselves and their students. It was amazing when, upon retirement, many teachers mentioned that they saved those notes.

SPOTLIGHT ON EFFECTIVE PRACTICE: IMMEDIATE FEEDBACK

Feedback practices should also be a part of the responsibility of teacher leaders, team leaders, coaches, and other administrators, and the feedback should extend beyond the formal evaluation procedures. Subject area leaders were required to meet twice each week with the principal to discuss curriculum concerns and best literacy practices across disciplines in an urban high school.

To share expertise among the group, they developed specific look-for criteria that were aligned with the school's vision and mission and that included classroom management techniques, instructional delivery strategies, and evidence of student engagement. This group then began scheduling observations among themselves to practice providing feedback regarding these look-fors, which impacted achievement. They were then more uniformly equipped and experienced to observe and provide feedback to other colleagues in and outside their content areas.

The feedback from these teachers included evidence-based suggestions to tweak planning, delivery, and follow-up to instruction. The results were significantly improved achievement by students in these leaders' classes. Another benefit was the additional expertise that these leaders developed, which were then applied to support their colleagues as they established observation and feedback sessions for the remaining members of the faculty. This teacher-to-teacher professional support was very powerful and became popular and valued among the entire faculty.

SPOTLIGHT ON EFFECTIVE PRACTICE: FEARLESS CONVERSATIONS

A high school principal had been working with one of his tenured social studies teachers for several months. He had observed her on several occasions, and she repeatedly used the same instructional methodologies from the previous observations. Her preferred method of teaching was lecturing students and rarely included

(Continued)

(Continued)

actively engaging them in their own learning. The principal provided opportunities for this social studies teacher to observe other teachers, gave her strategies to actively engage students, and modeled for her how to put those strategies into action. She was still resistant to changing her delivery of instruction.

Students were often found sleeping in her classroom, and she would continue talking as if she had their attention. During the past three years, this teacher had been in three different schools, and not one principal, for a variety of reasons, was able to document her deficiencies in instructional delivery. When she saw the writing on the wall at one school, she would apply for a transfer, and because the evaluation process was often cumbersome and ineffective, principals would grant her request. This principal decided to act differently.

He gave her multiple opportunities, resources, and supports to improve, and his recommendations fell on deaf ears. When he met with her for the post-observation conference, she immediately began to talk about what was wrong with her students as opposed to acknowledging any personal shortcomings as an instructor. The principal listened to her excuses, comments, and criticisms, recorded them in his notes, and formulated the specific feedback this teacher needed to hear from him. In addition, he was aware that after the first quarter of the year, she had the highest failure rates among her students who were demonstrating mastery in all their other classes.

She had been observed formally on two occasions and informally on five occasions by the principal and two assistant principals. All of these leaders documented the conversations they had with her, and all noticed a recurring pattern that was interesting. All noted the lack of growth or change, and all noted the offensive and sometime aggressive stance of the teacher during feedback conferences.

In framing the feedback she needed to receive this time, he said, "These are the areas of your instruction that continue to be of concern to me. Your planning and delivery still do not include meaningful activities to actively engage students, and it appears that there is no attempt to vary your instructional delivery. There is a decided lack of rigor or relevance in your instruction. After multiple feedback sessions, this leads me to conclude that there is an unwillingness on your part to try to do things differently. Every attempt has been made to assist you by providing you with a variety of instructional strategies and modeling them for you, sending you in with specific criteria to observe from highly successful teachers, and providing you with multiple digital and other resources. At this time, I must inform you that you are now on a formal plan of assistance, and you will have three months to turn this around. If there is no improvement, I will be making a recommendation for your termination. In addition, I will not approve any requests for you to transfer."

Summary

To make good progress, accurate, timely, and adequate feedback regarding current practices and protocols is essential. Well-planned and focused feedback provides guidance and direction to support ongoing needs and changes. Most schools and systems have numerous ways of collecting data and measuring and reporting progress. However, sharing and using the information in ways that help everyone to greater progress is not consistently practiced. Using appropriate feedback strategies that are targeted to current results allows stakeholders to develop or strengthen efforts and commitments to improving achievement.

Among the many realities that school leaders will face in their careers are the teachers who are willing and able, those who are willing and unable, those who are able and unwilling, and those who are unwilling and unable. The willing and able teachers are frequently treated as gifted students through an assumption that they do not have the need for significant feedback.

The reality is that this group of teachers with appropriate feedback, support, and encouragement very often will rise to incredible performance heights. These teachers are open to more and nurturing feedback, and when it is provided, they and their students soar. They are the ones to further develop their instructional leadership skills, to share their strengths with other faculty, and to model for other teachers.

Then there are the able and unwilling teachers. These are the teachers who have done the same things year in and year out. Sometimes they have taught students, parents, and others that they are "icons" among educators and protect themselves by assuming aggressive adversarial roles in unions and other organizations. This group is often harder to work with when trying to get them to attempt more effective strategies. These teachers generally know their content areas but are resistant to anything that resembles change. School leaders will find themselves spending a lot of time with this group in the hopes of turning their thinking around. The combination of persistence and patience is necessary for school leaders to have to work with this group.

Then there are the unwilling and unable, who will self-destruct as they attempt to pretend to care about more than just getting a paycheck. These are often short-timers who sometimes will not earn tenure or are sometimes evaluated out of the classroom. When these teachers slide under the radar, they can become the anchors that stop the boat from sailing smoothly unless they are placed on a plan of assistance. It is imperative that they are informed immediately that improvement is their best option.

Sometimes it just takes a school leader to initiate the sometimes difficult dismissal process with one or two of these folks, and some of the other non- or low performers will change their minds and behaviors. It is up to leaders who are willing to provide necessary feedback to help these teachers realize that resistance and incompetence will not be accepted, overlooked, or ignored. There are no secrets in schools regarding who is or who isn't pulling his or her own weight. It is damaging to leaders' credibility when these issues are not addressed.

Whatever category your teachers fall into, they all need honest, focused, and consistent feedback. As school leaders we need to strengthen cheerleading skills to encourage innovation and better ways to do things. In the absence of useful and appropriate feedback there will be a vast void between what is expected and what gets done in each school. We can't do more, but we can do better!

Reflections

The following questions are designed to provoke additional thinking and discussions about improving through effective feedback.

1. What is typical follow-up after feedback is given to stakeholders?

2. Do the data collected provide the most beneficial information that allows for planning for improvements?

3. When or how is fearless conversation initiated with individuals or groups of individuals who continuously refuse to change?

Chapter 4

Increasing Parent and Community Stakeholder Partnerships

> At the end of the day, the most overwhelming key to a child's success is the positive involvement of parents.
>
> —Jane D. Hull

Increasing the involvement of parent and community members is vital to school improvement for students and staff. Student achievement is enhanced and assured when school staffs work more effectively with parents. It is critically important to make schools feel like open, inviting, inclusive and friendly places for students, teachers, parents, and community members.

Although many of our schools already work hard to create and sustain that type of atmosphere for the students and faculty, frequently the same efforts are not applied as consistently to the inclusion and involvement of parents and other stakeholders. The impact that these stakeholders have on student achievement, the ultimate goal, requires greater consideration to be applied to this endeavor. Specific effort can and should be applied to encouraging parental and other community stakeholders to be included and more involved in a variety of ways.

Effective Communications and Community Outreach

One of the most important steps for leaders, as advocated by Robert Marzano, Willard Daggett, and Ronald Ferguson, among others, is to establish strong avenues of communications between the school and home and between the school and other stakeholders in the community. Experience has taught many leaders in today's schools that this includes consistently translating outgoing information in the multiple languages of the linguistically diverse students and community, using various methods of sharing outgoing information, and providing vehicles to generate feedback on the quantity and quality of that information. Taking advantage of popular, well-known digital, electronic, and social media resources such as Facebook, Twitter, and so on in today's world is a major cost-effective advantage.

It is helpful for leaders to use outreach initiatives. Sometimes the effort can be as simple as changing the venue for small meetings. For example, explore the possibilities in school neighborhood venues such as community or party rooms located in many apartment complexes as well as accessing community resource or service rooms in a local mall or shopping center. Parents may be more comfortable in these familiar surroundings because they are often more comfortable and consistent parts of their lives.

Let's not forget other community stakeholders who sometimes appreciate being involved beyond donating toward fund-raising activities. For example, an effective strategy could be approaching local corporations to partner with schools by requesting tutors and mentors or asking small businesses to lend employees to help chaperone and/or sponsor certain activities. Many larger businesses frequently have policies that allow employees to provide this type of outreach support to schools.

> *Parents and other community stakeholders need consistent, multiple, user-friendly, and comfortable ways to be involved in schools.*

In addition, parents and other community stakeholders need consistent, multiple, user-friendly, and comfortable ways to be involved in management, decision-making, and leadership opportunities at schools on a variety of levels. Frequently, school faculties have traditional ideas and strategies to engage in full partnerships with parents. An effective vehicle to use for change is to sponsor some focus groups to ask parents for their ideas on how to best to broaden the avenues of communications at their schools and how schools can help them develop a higher level of comfort and confidence with existing processes.

Addressing Resistance

Be prepared for resistance from several possible sources. In one school, the first resistance was anticipated somewhat, and it came from the parent sector. The ideas that were shared about deeper involvement were not particularly comfortable for several parents because they were not sure that they were prepared to fully participate. Some parents, mainly from the international communities, believed they would be intruding inappropriately by becoming more involved in school governance and decision-making. These ideas were culturally alien to what their understandings were about schooling. Some parents expressed skepticism by making comments such as "We send our children to you, the experts, and you are supposed to know what you are doing. Why do you need us to help you do your job?"

In addition, there are sometimes small groups of parents who may welcome the ideas because they believe they can create and sustain advantages for their children through this higher level of visibility. Sometimes these desired advantages are obvious when ideas and suggestions are promoted that clearly exclude other children. Leaders simply must acknowledge among themselves that these parents' motives are less than "pure" and make every effort to ensure that benefits suggested and incorporated from this group are advantageous to all children.

Some of the more surprising resistance can come from some of the faculty members. Again the ideas may not be within their comfort zones and will generate comments such as "We are doing fine without their (the parents) interference. They will just be here to spy on us." Some teachers believe that their experiences with parental input have been mostly negative and that parents in general are looking for ways to prove teachers are at fault for any problems that students may have at school. Their perspectives should not be minimized or negated because all personal experiences are valid, even when the perceptions and recollections of them are not entirely accurate. Numerous opportunities should be initiated that encourage staff and parents to get to know each other better, gain trust, and positively interact.

Other community members and organizations may not be resistant to the ideas as much as they may be reluctant to become involved at deeper and more meaningful levels. Time commitments that would be required are a major concern, and clarity of their roles in the process is another. Communicating the overall vision, benefits, and possibilities that could result from stronger alliances and partnerships will go a long way toward alleviating and dissolving those fears. Inviting, nurturing, and sustaining this involvement is a significant responsibility of local school leaders.

Increasing Stakeholder Involvement

It is in everyone's best interest to continue to explore strategies and ideas that facilitate increased involvement in ways that are positive, helpful, and sustainable. Many schools struggle with attempts to find solutions that work. Our students are the beneficiaries of our investment in successful strategies that work in K–12 schools and districts to enrich and strengthen our relationships and communications with parents and other community members. Exploring some nontraditional ideas and ways of building and sustaining these supportive relationships are critical.

Several types of partnerships are well worth the time and energy required to explore them further. There are traditional school-business partnerships and school–university partnerships. Each are often unique and designed to address a special need. However, most existing partnerships and new alliances can continue to address the needs for which they were originally designed as they expand to explore other ideas and creative options.

One example is that a partnership with a university, local or long distance, can yield numerous benefits to all stakeholders. The university benefits include increasing awareness and support for additional enrollment opportunities in course work for parents and teachers (perhaps even at reduced tuition rates) to develop new skills and/or pursue additional degrees and certifications. Schools and districts benefit by recruitment opportunities for future employees, increased student support from newly trained adults who are often excited about teaching, and increased student exposure to adults with additional talents that are grounded in current research, ideas, and protocols.

Ideas to Help Generate Involvement

Ideas for school leaders, administrators, and teachers to help generate better and often increased communications and support from parents and community members are as numerous as there are people. A few doable ideas and examples are brainstormed and explained here that are user-friendly and cost-effective in many schools and school systems. Most are stress free or require minimum additional effort. Most are also doable, adaptable, and practical at the elementary, middle, and high school levels.

Example 1

One example is when a high school created and hosted free family recreational activities on a monthly basis and invited everyone to participate in the event as a family. The school featured two gymnasiums from the days prior to Title IX, when we had a boys' gym and a girls' gym. These two large spaces were partitioned to feature activities that varied including billiards, basketball, Ping-Pong, badminton, line dancing, radio-controlled car races, and numerous other options that were of interest. The media center featured board and card games and tournaments as well as study supports. The laboratory formerly known as home economics featured child care sponsored by the student council association and activities that appealed to children five and under. The auditorium featured family-friendly videos with free popcorn sponsored by the parent–teacher association.

Example 2

Another example is when the mathematics department at a middle school decided to involve more parents by sponsoring Math Night. The teachers included suggestions from their students and even had some students participating as "teachers" and guides during the evening to help parents navigate the wide variety of stations that featured aspects of the mathematics curriculum for each grade level. Parents learned through simulations, demonstrations, modeling, and mini lessons what their children were expected to learn.

They included light refreshments, donated door prizes from local businesses, and numerous attractions that were extremely popular, making the activity a huge success. The results were that the investment of time and energy included greater understanding from the parent community to support the students. Mathematics scores soared on standardized testing, math competitions with other schools were a piece of cake, and other faculty members were motivated and encouraged to initiate more outreach opportunities for parents featuring their curricula.

Once data of achievement were shared with parents, they became more engaged in learning what teachers expected their children to know and be able to do, thus creating a new layer of support and encouragement in the home.

Once data of achievement were shared with parents, they became more engaged in learning what teachers expected their children to know and be able to do, thus creating a new layer of support and encouragement in the home. This simple, cyclical idea can be expanded to become a more frequent event and will work at every grade level.

Example 3

A middle school learned that one of the feeder elementary schools was letting younger children take folders or envelopes home on Fridays to their parents with the week's work enclosed. This invited greater two-way communication on the envelope or a preprinted form. The adaptation at the middle school was to declare Thursdays as Backpack Day. Students and parents understood that all correspondence from school, except emergency correspondence, would come home on Thursdays. Parents were encouraged to check backpacks for their contents and information. Students refrained from putting very private items in their backpacks on Thursdays.

Each student was given a large, brown envelope on Thursdays that they stuffed during the last three minutes of the day with newsletters, letters to parents, papers needing signatures, and so on.

On the rare Thursdays when there was nothing to send home, students were given a large, laminated pink card for their envelopes to announce there was no news this week. All envelopes were to return on Friday morning. Once everyone became used to the system, it was extraordinarily effective as even the bus drivers, secretaries, and custodians joined the efforts by urging students to not lose their envelopes on the journey home.

Teachers initially offered incentives and competitions to ensure the envelopes did not take up new residence on busses, in lockers, and in other unintended places. Also, on Backpack Day, there was a form that was included for parents to ask questions or state concerns, and teachers would respond promptly via a phone call or e-mail message when these forms were received. Thursdays were the best day to facilitate this activity in this community because it reduced weekend losses and was better timing to get information out. Again, the enhanced two-way communication was very rewarding for both parents and teachers.

Example 4

One high school established homework hotlines with tape-recorded messages that were used to remind youngsters of what their homework assignments were. A middle school offered a variation of the concept, called Homework Help Line. Because all students were issued a free planner to record homework and other events, they were taught and expected to record their homework and assignments in it from each class. Teachers who assigned homework would randomly check the planners to ensure compliance.

The help line was a designated telephone number that used call forwarding technology to roll the incoming call to whatever number was programmed to receive the call. Thus incoming calls were manned by staff or parents (paid for with grants or volunteers) to address students' homework support needs. The persons manning the calls had complete flexibility in choosing where to receive the calls during their duty time slots. This option removed the last excuse from students for not doing homework and became extremely popular, especially at examination and grading times.

The planners served as efficient communicating tools between teachers and parents as they could write notes to each other in the book. Additionally, the planners served the dual purpose of being used as hall passes when students were out of the classroom for any reason. This provided an additional incentive for students to retain their planners to use throughout the day even in classes that did not assign homework as planners became the only hall pass that was acceptable.

Example 5

A middle school used narrated slides or video presentations to orient parents and students to their school and their classrooms. The presentations were quickly and easily assembled by a tech-savvy volunteer: sometimes a yearbook staff member, a video club member, or another interested party. These were particularly helpful for orientations and for sharing achievement expectations and/or assisting parents in gaining familiarity with the physical school facilities, vision and mission of the school, special programs, and extracurricular activities. Additionally, these presentations could be copied on a CD and sent to feeder schools, and/or uploaded on YouTube, or linked the school's website, for those parents who were unable to attend meetings due to work schedules or family obligations with multiple children at different schools.

Example 6

One high school in northern Virginia with a very large, diverse population of non-English speaking families placed "WELCOME" signs at the entrance of the school in as many languages that were spoken at the school. Being culturally sensitive to your populations of students from diverse backgrounds is a powerful strategy to bring parents into schools, particularly those parents who feel underserved, overlooked, or who have not been traditionally invited to play an active role in the life of a school community.

In addition, signs identifying common areas or items are valuable and appreciated. Much of what we take for granted as English speakers is not always fully understood by others from other cultures. This particular high school found it helpful to post useful and discrete signs in multiple languages throughout the building that labeled water fountains, bathrooms, auditoriums, fire extinguishers, and so on. The cafeteria staff noticed an increase in sales and participation in the cafeteria when food items were labeled in a variety of languages. The custodians reported a dramatic improvement in the schoolwide recycling efforts when refuse containers, and their purpose and importance, were labeled in multiple languages.

All faculty and staff members need to explore strategies that increase transparency of schooling and that are inviting at all times. It is helpful when they greet parents and students in a friendly manner, and it is helpful to have faculty members' names and subject area(s) and/or grade levels posted on the doors of their classrooms. Common areas such as cafeterias, gyms, or auditoriums should have some form of invitations, acknowledgments, or appreciations for the diversity of the community and/or some visible sense of awareness that we all live in a global community.

Example 7

Aligned with example number one, another high school invited all students and parents new to the school to visit on a designated date prior to its opening for the school year. For those parents who did not have transportation, or were physically disabled, busses were provided to pick them up at the same location that their children were picked up during the school year.

For those parents whose first language was not English, translators were provided for them so they could understand everything and feel a part of the school community. In communities where it is appropriate, it is very positive to invite all participants to bring a traditional family dish for a potluck dinner to kick off this back to school event. Nothing brings people of different cultures together more than breaking bread together. However, food allergies and litigation in one community eliminated this option, so each family was encouraged to bring a picnic-style meal for their family, and the school sponsored and featured snacks, desserts, and beverages from its cafeteria. Many schools today offer pre-opening school activities that may include a free dance, a day of visitation to learn the layout of the facility, and an opportunity to meet many staff members.

One concern is the cost of providing transportation and translators to such an event. If this is a concern, then perhaps there is an opportunity for the school to solicit corporate sponsors or local businesses and organizations. Many major corporations have specifically designated resources for community projects, and schools are becoming increasingly popular to support through the growing recognition that they are also significant stakeholders for the future consumers and workforces locally, nationally, and internationally. In addition, community service agencies and small businesses often are interested in volunteer initiatives.

Civic organizations in many communities such as the Elks, Kiwanis, the United Way, and Rotarian Clubs often seek ways to support efforts by schools that are designed to boost achievement and that are inclusive of their school populations. Sororities and fraternities, particularly African American Greek letter organizations, are often service-driven groups that provide layers of support for school programs and initiatives. These groups adopt schools to support many of their improvement projects.

Let's not forget the faith community, which includes but is not limited to churches, mosques, and synagogues. These are organizations that are familiar with the needs of their congregants and are often eager to be included in helping parents become further involved in the lives of their children in their schools.

Example 8

Several schools have established opportunities for students in Grades 1 through 12 to develop pen-pal, digital, and other media-related relationships internationally with business leaders and other professionals in the community. Often there are individuals who, if invited, would love to communicate with and mentor students through informal notes, tweets, e-mails, letters, and other means. This has led to shadowing experiences for students who were pursuing particular careers or internships in which students were able to explore career opportunities.

These relationships can be established at an early age through the use of technological and digital means. However, this is an activity that needs to be closely monitored by parents, teachers, and potential candidates for these opportunities need to be diligently screened to ensure the safety of our children.

Example 9

In many middle and high schools, parents are invited to help with or organize both instructional and noninstructional activities. More than just participating in bake sales, candy sales, or other fund-raisers, parents can and should play essential roles in science fairs, as spelling bee judges, in book swaps, and as part of career-day workshops. Parents should also be encouraged to participate in the parent–teacher organizations or parent–teacher–student association groups and serve on or lead committees that allow them a more active voice in the life of the school.

Their perspectives can assist in multiple ways from planning international trips to serving on governance committees that help ensure that all students can participate regardless of their economic situations. Parents should also be encouraged to participate in booster organizations including academics, athletics, and the fine arts. In several schools a popular activity is a parent-sponsored athletic competition between students and staff or talent shows featuring students, parents, faculty, and administrators.

A thoughtful and inclusive-minded leader initiates, develops, and supports ways for all parents to participate.

Example 10

Several principals administer survey instruments to parents and faculty to assess the quality and degree of implementation of practices and activities to address key issues and policies. This is an effective way to determine the effectiveness of programs that are controlled by the faculty and administration. This is also a means of providing parents with a voice in school operations. Survey results are a culmination of data that can inform all stakeholders on the perceptions of how well overall school initiatives or school programs are perceived by parents.

For example, one of the authors was the principal of a new high school that wanted to eliminate lower-level classes that did not make instruction rigorous or relevant for students who learned differently. The other author was a newly appointed principal of an established high school that had been steeped in traditions of excellence, but academic achievement had declined over the years for a variety of reasons.

The principal of the new school made a policy decision to create honors, advanced placement, and academic-leveled classes and eliminate the lower-level tracking model that had been traditionally used within the district. The principal of the established school used a collaborative model of leadership among the faculty and parents to reestablish higher expectations by changing the status of the school to an advanced placement school. Both of these processes were successful because the leadership changed the achievement opportunities for students, and appropriate support was given to students by engaging parents and community shareholders.

In both of these circumstances, the principals found that the traditional schooling included too many students who were caught in a cycle of repeated failures. Both principals had the support of superintendents to implement changes that would increase achievement, particularly for underserved students. Yes, there were instances of parents and even faculty members who were not aligned with the visions that the principals had for the schools. They held valid but inaccurate fears were that students would ultimately be harmed and that teachers would be pressured to dummy down curriculum content for students who were not traditionally found in higher-leveled classes, among others.

The principal of both schools ensured quality professional development in advanced placement or honors-level instruction for teachers prior to the opening of school and throughout the school year. Data were collected weekly and monitored the successful progress of these initiatives. Parents were mostly very pleased with the results. The principal of the established school facilitated, site-based, and internally provided professional development along with the TLs and also collected and monitored the ongoing data. The results were considered extraordinary.

Example 11

One of the attributes of a highly successful school is the publication of a curriculum guide and activities calendar for the school year. Often these and many other school publications are featured on the school's website and other electronic media. A major advantage to utilizing electronic media is that it is a cost-effective means to allow each teacher to establish and maintain individual links that can include course syllabi, student achievement expectations, rubrics, and other classroom news. To keep parents involved they must be informed.

All school leaders should ensure that parents know what curriculum is being taught, when components are being taught, and what activities are designed to support the content acquisition throughout the year. Maintaining an activities and academic calendar should include important dates for parents, academic achievement updates, and all extracurricular and cocurricular events. These calendars should include the times and places for remediation and enrichment activities, testing dates, test preparation dates, and holidays.

Example 12

Highly effective principals and other leaders assume the responsibility of creating a consistently scheduled newsletter or bulletin to parents in print and digitally. This is a great means to provide timely updates, kudos, and recognitions for teachers, students, community groups, and other stakeholders. Multiple stakeholders can be encouraged and invited to contribute to its content. It can also be used to remind parents and all other stakeholders of upcoming events that are curriculum based and activities that will be taking place in the upcoming months. This is also another means to help keep parents focused on the vision and mission of the school and how they can support its success.

Example 13

Principals should develop positive ways to communicate with the local press to highlight aspects of school life or to generate an annual or quarterly special feature about the school. Keep in mind that you will never have to call the press when there is a fight at a football game or if there is a fire in a garbage can outside your building; they will know about it. The press is hardwired for disaster and negative stories because those sell media, especially on slow news days.

It is sometimes challenging to get good news published or featured about school, and thus, it helps to establish and maintain positive relationships with several reporters and their editors who cover the school beat. When achievement scores make exponential gains, or graduation rates increase toward 100 percent, or if there was a significant increase in students taking the advanced placement examinations receiving a 3 or better, it is a good idea to contact these individuals. Remember that the most important

It is sometimes challenging to get good news published about school, and thus it helps to establish and maintain positive relationships with reporters and stakeholders. The most important stories about school can come from parents and other stakeholders. They often have tremendous untapped clout and credibility with the press.

stories about school can come from parents and other stakeholders. They often have tremendous untapped clout and credibility with the press.

Having a parent liaison who can also work with the press is a positive way to get the good news out about school.

Caution! To avoid disciplinary or other actions that are potentially unpleasant, ensure compliance with school board policies and procedures for dealing with the press. Many school divisions have a designated person who handles the majority of the official communications with the press, and if this is the case, get to know him or her very well, and keep the information flowing.

Example 14

A good strategy to use that encourages and increases parental participation at many schools is to host or offer classes, seminars, or forums for parents on family issues that impact learning. In many schools classes are conducted for non-English-speaking parents in an effort to help them assist their children in completing assignments and to help them better communicate with teachers and other school personnel. The more diverse the population of the school, the more this service needs to be made available to non-English-speaking parents. Communication becomes the number one issue for these families who are new to the country and whose children are making both cultural and social adjustments.

In a middle school where one of the authors served, a survey of parents indicated that evening seminars on topics of strong interest to parents would be met with high enthusiasm. The survey also surprisingly indicated that Friday evenings were the favored timeframe. Presentations that were highly successful and were attended by 75 or more parents included, but were not limited to, How to Help Your Child With Homework, Ways to Help Your Child Stay Away From Drugs, and Identifying Signs of Depression From Other Adolescent Changes. Three wildly successful sessions that attracted more than 100 attendees included information on annual standards; in another, a panel of students told parents the things that some parents often do that annoy kids; and another featured the police showing ordinary household items that also double as drug paraphernalia.

For parents in general, whether English speaking or non-English speaking, they often need help in understanding adolescent behavior and the levels of support adolescent children need as they approach and go through puberty. Sessions on typical adolescent behavior are often a helpful offering to parents during the evenings or other convenient times. The level of understanding that parents need to have during these years with their children has a huge impact on the learning of their children. The social and emotional development of children during this period of their lives will determine their ability to cope with change, work with others and to prepare for the responsibilities required of global citizenship.

With the array of social and psychological issues that face our students and their families, specifically with teenage pregnancy and birth rates on the rise in many areas, it is extremely important to have parenting classes for those youngsters, along with their parents, who are now grandparents for the first time. Becoming a parent and attending high school, and in some cases middle school, seems impossible without appropriate support from the school and social agencies. Many of these students become dropouts because they have no viable support from their families, and in some cases these students are emancipated minors who have little or no support other than the school. For these youngsters it is even more important for the school to work closely with social services agencies to provide training for important prenatal care, giving birth, and the proper care of a newborn child.

Those students whose parents are incarcerated and may be in the custody of grandparents or other caregivers are frequently recruited by local gangs as a place to find familial ties, although these ties frequently have negative impacts and results. There are many who are reluctant to support school personnel becoming involved in these types of social interventions. However, we advocate walking the extra mile for students whenever it is necessary to increase achievement and reduce their dropping out of school.

Example 15

One strategy to further involve parents in the life of school is to sponsor periodic coffee or teas or other face-to-face events with parents and teachers. If a principal makes a concerted effort to dedicate a full day each semester for parents to visit and talk with him or her in an open forum, also attended by teachers during part of their planning period, that would create another opportunity for collaborative interaction with the principal and the school community. Having a time to listen to the concerns of school stakeholders is a skill that if mastered, will lead to unprecedented support. Additionally, this is a time for brainstorming ideas that will make the school a better place for students and the community at large. Offering coffee, tea, fruit, and donuts periodically is a small price to pay for providing access and keeping a community informed and involved in the life of your school.

Summary

This chapter discussed numerous reasons to eliminate the undervaluing of parent partnerships and the benefits that are insufficiently harvested from stronger community involvement in our schools. It also distinguishes the differences between including and involving these stakeholders. The authors discussed several powerful strategies that go well beyond the traditional fund-raising, donations, and hospitality roles that schools often assign to parents and community organizations and, thus, underutilize their potential to positively impact student achievement improvement goals.

The examples shared are not an exhaustive list, but they are a beginning to anchor thinking about the types of ways to engage parents and community stakeholders more productively in school operations. Based on the U.S. Department of Education, National Center for Educational Statistics (1998), some of the greatest barriers to parent involvement are encountered by schools and districts serving low-income households, racial or minority students, and students with limited English proficiency. Again, readers are invited to share successful examples with the authors.

Reflections

The following questions are designed to provoke additional thinking and discussions about increasing parent and community stakeholder partnerships.

1. What actions are required to engage and involve the hardest-to-reach parents and community stakeholders in our school and district?

2. What are three activities or strategies that I can do immediately to increase the level of participation of parents and community stakeholders in our school and district?

3. How are we assessing the areas of inclusion and involvement of parents and community stakeholders? How and what are we communicating to the community?

Chapter 5

Managing and Sustaining an Organized, Productive, Ever-Changing School Culture

> An educational system isn't worth a great deal if it teaches young people how to make a living but doesn't teach them to make a life.
>
> —Author Unknown

The term *school culture* generally refers to the beliefs, norms, values, perceptions, relationships, and attitudes, which include written and unwritten rules and expectations that shape and influence every aspect of how a school or organization functions. In other words, it's how we do business around here. However, the term also encompasses more concrete issues such as the physical and emotional safety of students, the orderliness of classrooms and public spaces, and the degree to which a school embraces and celebrates racial, ethnic, linguistic, and/or cultural diversity.

Like the larger social cultures, a school culture evolves from both conscious and unconscious perspectives, values, interactions, and practices, and it is heavily influenced by a school's particular institutional history. Students, parents, teachers, administrators, and other stakeholders all contribute to their school's culture, as do other influences such as the community in which the school is located, the policies that govern how it operates, or the principles upon which the school was founded (Great Schools Partnership, 2013).

Defining and Articulating School Culture

Understanding the definition of school culture is only the beginning of understanding how leaders manage, nurture, and sustain it. Let's imagine that you are opening a new school. What are the first steps in building a strong school culture? How do you address toxicity in a culture?

Step 1. Do not assume that you know and understand the culture of your school community.

Do your homework. Identify the socioeconomic, political, religious, and demographic factors that are significant or may affect the school. Learn who the power brokers are and what and who they influence in the school. Determine the involvement of civic organizations in the school and how active they are in the community.

Too often school leaders have false assumptions about their school communities, which can result in major conflicts during their tenures. What school leaders often find is that the most vocal parents and community members are also the most affluent and are accustomed to having the most influence on matters of interest to them. Although they are important, leaders must also pay attention to the more silent segments of school communities that are often underserved and overlooked. All stakeholders must have a viable presence and voice in their school.

Although vocal parents and community members are important, leaders must also pay attention to the more silent segments of school communities that are often underserved and overlooked. All stakeholders must have a viable presence and voice in their school.

Sometimes to ensure equitable participation and a sense of belonging by everyone, the effort required is as simple as inviting stakeholders to the school to participate in various ways. Another strategy to accomplish this goal is to make home or neighborhood visits to access families who do not traditionally or typically participate in their children's education. For example, one principal asked a Somalian family to invite neighbors and friends who had children in her school to meet several key school leaders for coffee at their home.

The principal attended the event along with four teacher leaders (TLs) and began building strong foundations of trust and mutual interest. The results were a very high degree of comfort from that part of the community. After attending the event, these families and their friends became more visibly involved with school functions and activities at or sponsored by the school. Meeting with underrepresented members of the school community on their turf will frequently provide more access and increase communication on multiple levels.

Another example is when a newly appointed principal asked students in her school where they worshipped, shopped, and hung out for recreational activities. She then asked a few students to if it was OK with them for her to visit their church services, and a date was agreed upon. Understanding protocols of services in many Baptist churches, she knew that a part of the services included an introduction of visitors, which would give her an opportunity to share who she was and to strengthen her relationships with her students. This, of course, led to other students and faculty members extending invitations to church, family, and community functions, which she attended as often as she could. Many in the international community were especially appreciative of her presence at their events.

Meeting with stakeholders is tremendously important. For example, another principal hosted an evening reception for local real estate agents and brokers that featured a video presentation of the exciting life in his school. Tours, a questions-and-answer dialogue, and folders with vital statistics were provided, were highly beneficial, and provided accurate, personable, and meaningful information. The results were that some incoming families reported that their agents were highly complementary and informative about the benefits of attending the school.

The reality was that real estate brokers recognized the importance of the quality of schools that were in proximity to the properties they listed on the market for sale. They were cognizant of how perceptions of the school impacted the values of homes in the neighborhood. Developing relationships with these kinds of stakeholders in the school community are often extended by partnerships that allow students to explore careers in these businesses and by having local businesses members mentor students who are interested in those career pathways. Meeting groups of these and other stakeholders in community centers or in churches also are viable means to engage a segment of school communities who might not traditionally play a visible or active role in the local school.

Sometimes unknown to school leaders is the extent of the numbers of homes within their school communities that include families who are struggling. They can include single-parent homes; homes where both mothers and fathers are having difficulty making ends meet and are unable to provide the minimal essentials for their children—food, clothing, and medical support; homes that have grandparents and aunts and uncles in custodial roles for the children of incarcerated parents; homes in which students have two moms or two dads in other nonconventional home environments; and a number of students who are homeless or who live in temporary shelters. It is important to know the primary stakeholders and how their social or economic statuses impact the culture of each school. School leaders must be willing and able to ensure that schools are welcoming and inviting places for all students, parents, and community stakeholders to share, invest, and engage in multiple important roles.

As former high school principals, both authors determined that it was important periodically to take their faculties and staff on community field trips during one of the professional development training days prior to the opening of the school year. It was important for the staff to physically see the diversity of housing, businesses, incarceration facilities, and other community elements that supported or impacted the students and families. It was always interesting to debrief with faculty and staff after the respective field trips and discuss ways to make the school a more productive, caring, supportive, and responsive learning environment.

It was also eye-opening for many staff members who simply never thought of where students lived and why it was important that school staff know this information. In one school, after the first field trip, the mantra of the school among the staff became "All Students First in All that We Do." The principals made it even clearer to all faculty and staff that any decision that was to be made had to be in the best interest of all kids.

SPOTLIGHT ON EFFECTIVE PRACTICE: CULTURE-BUILDING STRATEGY

It is essential that school leaders recognize and take action to build strong, positive, and inclusive school cultures that acknowledge that although what and how we teach is important, it is critically important

(Continued)

(Continued)

to know who we teach. For example, in each grade level assembly on opening day, one principal, announced to the approximate 950 students that by winter break, he would know all their names and one thing about each one of them. He further captured their interest by telling them that if he didn't know their names and at least one thing about them by the deadline, then he would buy those students lunch for the remainder of the school year. The only rule was that they had to provide their correct name when asked in each encounter.

Following the principal's lead, this encouraged students and teachers to get to know each other, even when they were not in the same classrooms. This modeling encouraged support staff, cafeteria workers, and maintenance personnel to do the same. The principal, students, and staff took great pride in his never having to purchase a single lunch for anyone.

The adults in that building knew not only the names of the students they taught but also the names of students they didn't teach or interact with on a daily basis. This was the foundation of building a strong school culture at that school and the foundation of building a strong, caring school community. For several generations of siblings and family members, this practice continued and helped shape the culture of this school for several years after the principal retired.

Changing the Culture

Step 2. Open multiple lines of communication, and develop expectations and nonnegotiables.

Whereas it is more challenging to teach those whom one does not know well, the same reasoning applies to school leaders as they are far more effective when they know their stakeholders well. Knowing them well is a foundation to good communications, and it is the responsibility of principals and other leaders to develop and initiate the communication processes. Opening and maintaining these communications requires all school leaders to consistently articulate the mission of the school to stakeholders, which reinforces common understandings about the purpose for schooling. It is equally important to ensure that all are knowledgeable about the expectations and nonnegotiables, such as safety and security.

Principals and other leaders of highly effective schools know that most effective communications often begin with face-to-face dialogues and meetings with stakeholders. These meetings should be consistent and can be one-on-one, with large- or small-group exchanges.

The initial agendas should address rationales for policy and other changes.

SPOTLIGHT ON EFFECTIVE PRACTICE: BUILDING CULTURE IDEA

In one high school the leadership team spent time discussing ways to address adults in the building and each other as a part of setting the tone at the beginning of the school year. The decision was made that behaviors of common courtesy and politeness were foundational expectations for all in the school environment.

To kick this policy off, the principal posted huge photographic display in the main hallway that featured ethnically diverse races of people. At the top of the picture was the Golden Rule, "Do unto others as you would have others do unto you." Every day this was the first thing that students saw when they entered the school, and displaying this photograph was the beginning of setting a tone for behavioral expectations that helped create a culture of cooperation and caring within the school.

Conversations about this policy was held with staff members to remind them that all adults in the building were expected to always model the behavior that they wanted students to emulate.

(Continued)

(Continued)

Demonstrating appropriate communication skills was required for all teachers along with the expectation that they follow the same rules for behavior and dress.

Some principals avoid addressing how adults dress in their schools, but this principal did, and he asked teachers to consider what the impact of conscious and unconscious, first and lasting, impressions was on students from adults wearing professional attire. Agreements were made, despite a variety of opinions, with his staff defining appropriate dress for their school. A compromise was reached that featured business casual attire from Monday through Thursday and a dress-down day on Friday.

The results were amazing. From the beginning, teachers expressed feeling good about themselves as they complimented each other throughout the day on how good they looked. It also got the attention of the students as they began seeing teachers looking differently than they did in the past. Parents and community members visiting the school praised the principal and the staff on how professional they looked every day and how their kids noticed this change. This cultural change resulted in a significant shift in the mind-sets and attitudes of teachers, students, and parents.

This principal believed that leaders should not be afraid to tackle unpopular issues. Some schoolwide rules can create difficult issues for both students and teachers. He knew that to create and sustain an organized and ever-changing culture, certain expectations were required and that the language used to articulate those expectations was important. Although some school leaders believe they need to communicate a laundry list of rules to define the culture and the daily operations of their schools, his perspective was that communicating two ideas would be sufficient.

These ideas were to clearly express expectations and nonnegotiables for behaviors, communications, symbols, new traditions, and customs. Cultural expectations are those values and beliefs about desired behaviors that are fostered in the learning environment. Nonnegotiables are those uncompromisable standards and norms of the culture. Each of these has consequences that manifest themselves in how a schools, departments, or teams function. Table 5.1 was the result of their collective efforts.

Within the first month of using the ideas in the table at school, there was a distinctive positive impact. This school recorded the lowest number of disciplinary referrals, suspensions, and reprimands to

[To be] most effective, these expectations, nonnegotiables, and consequences should not be developed solely by the principal but through significant input from stakeholders.

Table 5.1. Student and Staff Expectations, Nonnegotiables, and Consequences

Expectations	Positive and Negative Consequences	Uncompromisable Standards	Positive and Negative Consequences
Being respectful and courteous to others	Praise and trust among teachers and peers	Foul language, racial slurs, disrespect, fighting, and other disruptive behavior.	Counseling, in-school or after-school detention, or suspension
Being to every class, every day on time	Rewards and privileges	Cutting classes	For students— parental contact and loss of privileges; for teachers— warning, reprimand, letter in personnel file

(Continued)

Table 5.1. (Continued)

Expectations	Positive and Negative Consequences	Uncompromisable Standards	Positive and Negative Consequences
Being respectful and courteous to others	Praise and trust among administrators, students, parents, and peers	Singling out and publicly embarrassing or bullying others	For students—meeting with administrator, in-school or possible out-of-school suspension; for teachers—formal reprimand or letter in personnel file
Being prepared for daily instruction	High student achievement, recognition from administration and peers	Not being prepared daily	Peer coaching, discussion with administrator, plan of assistance

teachers ever in the history of this school. All members of this school community took on the challenge of creating a strong and positive school culture. Tables like this can be created by student councils and principal advisory groups.

What may be different and most effective is that these expectations, nonnegotiables, and consequences should not be developed solely by the principal but through significant input from stakeholders. Sometimes leaders become embroiled in serving agendas and protocols that have nothing to do with serving kids. Politically, it is sometimes challenging to do the right things as opposed to doing things right.

One of the biggest obstacles to overcome as a leader is to know when and how to get out of the way of other stakeholders who should and often would like to contribute. It is more important for leaders to remain focused on the destinations while ensuring that the stakeholders have choices and/or input on the pathways of the journey. When this happens, stakeholders are most likely to exceed expectations and enculturate the nonnegotiables.

SPOTLIGHT ON EFFECTIVE PRACTICE: MANAGING CULTURE, CONFLICT, AND DIVERSITY

A highly ethnically and culturally diverse urban high school principal had increasing concerns about neighborhood gang activities and presence at multiple school events. Students were becoming more polarized by wearing their colors and other paraphernalia to school community events. Realizing that her primary responsibility was the safety and security of all 2,000 staff, students, and other stakeholders who were on campus daily, she knew a policy change was required that would change portions of traditions that were valued in the current school culture. The principal was also fully aware of the impact that changes often have on stakeholders and that sometimes perceptions are more important than facts. Many stakeholders at the school were very proud and protective of the current culture, believing that it was inclusive, stable, and anchored in strong values, beliefs, and norms.

However, closer examination of the culture revealed that the perceptions were no longer as accurate as they had been in the past. Suspension data were high, achievement data were low, attendance was declining, and students participating in the arts, athletics, and other extracurricular activities were low too. Clearly, changing the culture needed to be a foundational component to

(Continued)

(Continued)

a school improvement plan to ultimately address overall needs for learning.

The principal and school leaders determined that the first and most feasible place to begin was to limit access to the campus by identified gang members while simultaneously changing the dress code to eliminate wearing headgear other than for religious reasons or having displays or possession of gang insignia on campus. On a campus that included 99 nations, it was a challenge to clarify what was culturally significant versus what was gang related.

However, through the use of numerous strategies that were designed and enforced by the stakeholders, this policy became very effective within two months of the new school year. The climate within the school changed to a more positive tone; stakeholders in focus groups expressed less fear and more positive feelings about the school. Disciplinary data declined, and participation increased in many clubs and activities. Attendance and academic achievement issues required other changes, but the groundwork had been laid, and stakeholders were more excited to thoughtfully consider other changes that could possibly lead to greater success.

Success does breed more success!

Most school systems have specific guidelines, policies, and/ or regulations that govern the behavior of both students and employees. However, when changing, developing, and growing a strong school culture, it is critical to include and involve all stakeholders in the process. What we have learned is the importance of active engagement by these stakeholders enriches trusting and collegial relationships within the school. These relationships are foundations of strong school cultures. There will certainly be some challenges when implementing this model, but ongoing and open dialogue will facilitate improvements.

Communicating the important attributes of healthy cultures requires the use of webinars, newsletters, social media, and other tools. Consistent communications about who we are, why we're here, and what's important to us is important in building and sustaining the values and norms. Those who speak languages other than English should have this communication translated to their dominant languages to enable them to be a part of the culture of each school.

Sustaining the Culture

Step 3: Monitor Instruction: Inspect What You Expect.

The act of managing while walking around with a focus is an essential visibility tool in creating, maintaining, and sustaining a strong school culture. As school leaders there is a strong need to be visible, accessible, and flexible. An instructional leader is less effective when he or she remains in the office. Visible and accessible leaders greet students, teachers, and support staff when they arrive in the mornings and often see them leave in the afternoon. In addition, effective instructional leaders also encounter and observe them in classrooms, activities, and common areas throughout the day. Too many leaders remain in their offices or work spaces, and other stakeholders seldom see them during the day.

One way leaders can avoid this trap is to plan each day around monitoring and observing instruction. The first stop in the morning after the first bell should be in a classroom, whether it is a walk-through or informal or formal observation. It helps to plan daily to walk a different route in the building (unless one is assigned to a specific area) and ensure that throughout the week, every classroom has been visited. If there are disciplinary or other more important and time-sensitive issues, take the referrals and/or your tablet with you. When entering classrooms, it is sometimes very convenient to also observe the behavior of referred students, and between classes, notes and responses can be made on tablets.

It is usually convenient and wise to briefly meet with students outside classrooms, address minor issues, and promptly return them to their classroom, reducing the loss of instructional time. While on patrol, it is also frequently convenient to meet briefly with teachers and other staff during their noninstructional times. When leaders spend the majority of their time in classrooms instead of their offices, there is often improvement in instructional delivery, student engagement, and student discipline. Students and teachers respond positively to the presence of administrators and other leaders when those presences are a natural and consistent part of the culture; when these visits are a part of supportive efforts to help with good instruction, the culture is strengthened.

Ray McNulty (2016), senior fellow of the International Center for Leadership in Education, said, "Culture is the set of habits that allows a group of people to cooperate by assumption rather than by negotiation." Those assumptions are a collective belief that is significant as part of a caring and nurturing learning environment where all are valued.

Dr. McNaulty (2016) gives us five steps to developing a successful culture. Step 1 is to be accountable to each other and ourselves. The phrase "It takes a whole village . . ." applies here. Having a collective vision for each school, as mentioned earlier, is what all members of the school community need to be accountable for, individually and collectively.

Step 2 is taking ownership of the outcomes. If the achievement and performance outcomes are lower than they should be, it is the responsibility of the entire village to turn it around. All must be a part of the solution and share ownership of fixing problems.

Step 3 is having or developing a commitment to achieve more each day and to be better each day. Teachers having a commitment to all students and students having a commitment to increasing and improving their own learning ensure that everyone achieves better and more. This is a powerful ingredient for building a strong school culture.

Step 4 is to work together as suggested by the marine core slogan "gung ho." Working together to each achieve more (t.e.a.m.) is essential for significant progress. Everyone needs to be valued and have opportunities to contribute. It reminds us of the saying "More than one head is good even when one is a cabbage head."

Step 5 is having the will to continue pressing forward when change gets difficult. This reminds us about the quote from another unknown author: "It's not that some people have will-power and some people don't. It's that some people are ready to change and others are not." Leaders must commit to working with both groups, ready or not.

In his own words, Dr. McNaulty (2016) said, "Changing is difficult, not changing is fatal." In other words, if we continue to do the same things that are not working, we will get the same results. He also stated, "Almost everyone wants schools to be better, but fewer want schools to be different." With so many competing demands on schools and school districts, with the implementation of new reforms, challenges abound for all leaders. Seymour Sarason (2002), school reform researcher said, "If you attempt to implement reforms but fail to engage the culture of a school, nothing will change."

To recognize and address toxic elements in a school's culture, leaders must be vigilant and consistently involved in monitoring and supporting all aspects of the school's culture. For smaller schools whose personnel generally must wear multiple hats while still accomplishing the same requirements as their larger counterparts, this is often more challenging than others realize. Frequently leaders will forego regular meetings with colleagues, making these low priorities for a variety of reasons. In actuality, prioritizing the consistency of these sessions is extremely

Prioritizing the consistency of collegial leadership sessions is extremely beneficial and goes a long way when used effectively toward building and strengthening a culture that is congruent with high student achievement.

beneficial and goes a long way when used effectively toward building and strengthening a culture that is congruent with high student achievement.

A useful tool that provides information that can help fully develop and/or change a school's culture is the Daggett System for Effective Instruction Readiness Rubrics (Daggett, 2015). These rubrics tools, reprinted with permission, can assist in answering some difficult questions about a school's culture in the areas of organizational leadership, instructional leadership and teaching. See Appendix A.

Summary

Many leaders benefit from a review of the distinctions between managing and leading and how these differences and similarities make an impact on our daily practices and overall job satisfactions. In this chapter the authors also discussed the impact of moving from traditional to transformational leadership to instructional leadership activities that will sustain a positive school culture. The commonsense approaches and examples provided by the authors can help improve the quality of school life for students, faculty, and staff.

In today's multidirectional climates, some leaders are too often more concerned with being politically correct than with paying more attention to fairness, equity, and diversity. This causes many to miss the mark in developing, growing, and improving their school cultures, which are essential to perpetual improvement, growth, and achievement. Hopefully this chapter will spark more usable ideas for discussions in framing a rationale for doing the right thing instead of just doing things right. These are the actions of leaders who are fearless in managing and sustaining an organized, productive, and ever-changing school culture.

Reflections

The following questions are designed to provoke additional thinking and discussions about managing and sustaining an organized, productive, ever-changing school culture.

1. What strategies or resources are needed to assess our school's and district's culture?

2. As a school or district leader, what skills are needed to improve and successfully manage and/or sustain positive components of the school's and district's culture?

3. What are the expectations for students, teachers, parents, and stakeholders for managing and owning the school's and district's culture? And what are our collective responsibilities for doing so?

4. How are we helping stakeholders adapt to, embrace, support, and/or initiate needed changes?

Chapter 6

Boosting Collegial Climates by Providing Embedded Professional Development

> The climate in a school can either make everything possible or not make everything possible.
>
> —Unknown

When faculty, staff, and students work in a supportive and collaborative environment, they strive to ensure that everyone is successful. This is the nucleus of a powerfully collegiate climate. The climate aspect of a school's culture is too often a low priority for the attention it needs to thrive, and in many cases, it is not addressed at all. Leaders are primarily responsible for establishing healthy climates.

Successful climates are anchored in collaborative decision-making, inspirational, and motivational recognition of stakeholders' achievements, and clearly defined, high performance expectations throughout the culture. In addition, it is essential that all stakeholders have clear opportunities to learn and grow.

Successful school climates are anchored in collaborative decision-making, inspirational, and motivational recognition of stakeholders' achievements and clearly defined, high performance expectations throughout the culture.

Creating and sustaining a strongly positive, supportive, and collaborative climate that perpetually sustains and renews itself requires multiple leaders who share the same vision, willingness, and commitment to the well-being, improvement, and growth of the school. This unified energy needs to be focused on creating and sustaining the following for all stakeholders:

- A sense of clarity and transparency

- An agreed-upon focus

- Performances anchored in standards

- Attitudes of flexibility and support

- Acknowledgments, recognition, and rewards

A sense of clarity and transparency involves leaders ensuring that all stakeholders know the expectations, mission, and vision and how their performance is tied to intended results. Teachers and support staff members flourish when they are provided the appropriate autonomy to make decisions and carry them out. Leaders must have clear and challenging goals for school personnel's performances and must inspire peak performances by connecting employees to their work emotionally and intellectually.

Leaders who communicate these expectations clearly and consistently can usually see solid links between a faculty's and staff's daily work and the progress toward the school's and district's goals. Fostering a sense of efficacy helps create a strong sense of ownership from these stakeholders.

SPOTLIGHT ON EFFECTIVE PRACTICE: Y'ALL COME MEETINGS

A high school principal wanted to encourage his administrative team and faculty members to initiate good ideas and assume responsibility for some of the professional development in the school instead of waiting to be asked. In an effort to let his administrative team, faculty, and staff understand this further, he called a special 10-minute faculty meeting at the end of the day. He announced, "I don't believe that I am the smartest person in this school. I lead, but I don't lead alone. Every one of you has leadership skills and additional potential, and to that end I want to start a new kind of idea exchange. It's called a 'Y'all Come Meeting.'"

He announced, "If any one of you has a good idea that you think will improve instruction, the work environment, or professional development, or even if you want to conduct a book study, you can count on me to announce and facilitate a session within five days. I only ask that the topic or topics of the sessions are aligned with improving our school and that you outline an agenda for those meetings." This announcement produced a range of responses from skepticism to expressions of excitement.

After a week, a social studies teacher, Ms. Johnson, approached him and requested to have a Y'all Come Meeting to discuss the formation of a student mentoring program. She had bounced this idea around several teachers who were interested and thought she would give it a try. The following morning an announcement was made that the first Y'all Come meeting would take place the next day after school; the topic would be developing a teacher/student mentor program.

(Continued)

(Continued)

To the surprise of the principal, the next day more than half of the staff showed up for the meeting. Ms. Johnson was a second-year teacher, but she was highly respected by her peers for having a great rapport with her students. She handed out her agenda and led the participants in a very engaging discussion about the formation of a mentoring program.

Within three weeks this group met several times and had designed a student mentoring program that would allow every student in the school to have at least one adult in the building whom they could go to for counseling or support in addition to their regular classroom teachers or counselor. The only request from this group was that the administrative team adjust the daily schedule to include a 45-minute block of time for teachers to meet with their mentees once a month. Because each week there was a 45-minute block of time dedicated to club participation and remediation activities, it was not hard to use one of those times to adjust for this new activity.

The principal asked one question of the group: What if there are teachers who do not want to participate? The results were that this group of teachers made such a great presentation to the faculty and staff that there was 100 percent participation. The principal simply got out of the way and let this wonderful thing happen.

Although it might have seemed that the principal took a risk, this leap of faith opened the door to more Y'all Come Meetings. The results were that teachers designed popular book studies, and they developed well-attended professional development activities about instruction, teacher leadership, and student engagement.

This principal developed another level of leadership in his staff that supported peer-to-peer coaching and professional development activities. All of these initiatives resulted in a stronger and more positive school climate and culture.

Sharing a Singular Focus

Far too often, school leaders try to solve all of the instructional issues within their schools all at once. We recommend an investment of sufficient time to analyze and reflect upon data as it will result in better instructional decisions. In managing the decision-making process, it is important for school leaders and their staffs to have a unified focus on the priorities and collaborative agreements on what to do about them. Whereas some would argue that the job requires managing multiple tasks at all times, as school leaders we must remember, as the saying goes, "The best way to eat an elephant is still one bite at a time."

SPOTLIGHT ON EFFECTIVE PRACTICE: READING ACROSS CONTENT AREAS

A high school principal and her leadership team met to discuss their achievement data from the previous school year. They discovered through the data that the common denominator for the lower levels of achievement was *reading* across all content areas. They then researched several programs that could possibly help improve reading skills. They determined that Creating Independence Through Student Owned Strategies (CRISS) was their best option to meet their students' needs. Training was arranged to teach teachers a variety of reading strategies that could be implemented in each content area most days in their classrooms.

During the two days of training, teachers became more excited about the reading strategies that they learned. The presenter modeled the strategies and gave teachers an opportunity to practice the use of these strategies with their peers. Following the professional development, a review of schoolwide lesson plans included evidence of multiple reading strategies being used

(Continued)

(Continued)

in every content area. Teachers began planning together and modeling strategies for each other to become more proficient in those strategies that they had difficulty with implementing. At the end of the school year, there was exponential growth in reading in all grade levels and in all subject areas.

The singular focus of this school was "All Hands on Deck" to improve reading throughout the school. This initiative was a major cultural shift that changed several significant aspects of daily school life. Professional development practices changed to become more collaborative, and communications among staff changed to become more focused on how to help kids. In addition, student attitudes toward school became more positive, and even student athletic and other competitions changed as critical thinking skills improved and teams began winning matches, games, and meets.

Performance Standards and Training

Climate and culture are often influenced by new and exciting ideas and strategies that help accomplish school goals. This is perhaps the best kind of professional development that can occur in any school as it becomes an ongoing part of the culture of collaboration and cooperation among teachers to benefit their students.

When leaders anchor performances in standards using goals that are challenging yet attainable, the results are spectacular. This requires leaders to regularly review faculty and staff's collective and individual performances. Consistently holding high performance standards for teachers will often push them to achieve their best work for students.

Leaders achieve best results when they encourage people to initiate tasks and projects they think are important and that are aligned with the vision and mission of the school and district. This creates trustworthiness among the stakeholders and helps in the appropriate use of the available resources to achieve intended achievement results.

SPOTLIGHT ON EFFECTIVE PRACTICE: PERFORMANCE STANDARDS

A school district's leadership team believed that when performance standards were used to attain goals in the classroom, the results would be better than in the previous years. They decided to address the absence of performance standards in their district to achieve positive academic results. They also decided that it was important to align those performance standards to the vision of the school division, "The academic achievement of ALL students," and thus began a conversation about collective and individual teacher performance.

They began looking at grade-level data, school by school, teacher by teacher, and subject by subject. At each grade level and school, there were teachers who needed additional support. The data revealed a lack of alignment or consistent focus across classrooms. Some teachers were doing well with certain populations of students, whereas others were doing poorly with the same students. A part of the problems was that here were no consistent performance standards within course contents, across grade levels, or among schools.

The superintendent then decided to conduct a series of focus groups anchored to one main question: "What are we individually and collectively responsible for if the academic achievement of *all* students is our goal?" In the several focus group sessions, there was agreement on the need to research current practices that would assist teachers to be more skillful at their craft and at the same time develop performance standards that could be observed and measured. Based on the work of Saphier and Gower's (1997) *The Skillful Teacher*, the leadership team of the school division adopted several performance standards.

The first of the top four performance standards was for teachers to demonstrate knowledge of content and curriculum. Each teacher

(Continued)

(Continued)

was responsible for understanding and utilizing the state standards and essential skills needed to teach all students in their disciplines and grade levels. Teachers had the responsibility of keeping abreast of current research and strategies in their content areas that would positively impact student achievement. Teachers also had to highlight the relationship between concepts taught and students' current knowledge.

Teachers were also required to better manage instruction for students by providing them with appropriate learning experiences, including independent study, small-group projects, or large-group discussions. Students would then be brought together to review and reflect upon their learning and have an opportunity to ask questions for clarification. They would also have an exit ticket to complete that would let the teacher know what they learned or show that students had completed a project or had an opportunity to ask questions that were not answered during the course or the lesson.

The third performance standard was teachers being responsible for managing student behavior by establishing and administering a consistent and fair set of rules that supported appropriate expectations. This resulted in students being more involved in the process of establishing classroom rules and expectations as a means to have them accountable for the rules that they helped create.

Teachers were held accountable for monitoring and evaluating student outcomes as a fourth performance standard. This resulted in more focused professional development anchored in differentiated instruction to ensure more effective and efficient instruction, assessment, and enrichment.

One thing that the superintendent and his leadership team realized was that consistent and ongoing training was necessary to address these performance standards. The training began with all of the administrators in the school division. Administrators had to understand what skillful teaching looked like before they could hold teachers accountable to these standards.

Every administrator had to go through extensive training before this was launched in schools. Once launched at the school level, teachers were provided with the standards and the training to go along with the standards.

In large measure performance standards give school divisions and individual schools the organizational structure necessary for the successful operation of schools and the behavior of all participants in the school community. These standards need to be communicated to all.

Flexibility as a Strength

Leaders who exhibit attitudes of flexibility are usually leaders who minimize and reduce unnecessary rules, policies, and procedures for leading and managing their schools and districts. This requires a regularly scheduled review of existing rules, policies, and procedures to ensure relevancy. This review also helps new leaders better understand historical perspectives and growth at their sites.

Another essential element of flexibility is conducting team, department, grade-level, and so on, meetings that serve to increase trust and mutual respect among stakeholders. A common mistake by many school leaders, particularly new leaders or leaders at smaller sites, make is to eliminate these meetings because many people just don't like them or perceive any relevance. It is incumbent upon primary leaders to make these occasions important, interesting, and useful enough to

It is incumbent upon primary leaders to make these occasions important, interesting, and useful enough to persuade people that these meetings are opportunities to collaborate within the school and district.

persuade people through the sessions that these meetings are opportunities to collaborate within the school and district. These sessions foster a feeling of belonging to an organization that is characterized by cohesion, mutual support, trust, and pride—all the foundation of a strong sense of community. They are also a significant form of ongoing professional growth and alignment.

SPOTLIGHT ON EFFECTIVE PRACTICE: DO YOU HAVE TOO MANY RULES?

A new principal in a high school in a small, urban city quickly realized that there were a lot school and classroom rules that were not enforced regarding student behavior. The leadership style of the former principal and his four assistant principals was more reactive than proactive, focused on putting out fires rather than fire prevention.

The previous principal was an unknown entity to students—they did not know his name. The new principal had only a few weeks to develop a different perception of how things would be changing. During the first meeting with his assistant principals, he asked them to describe the schoolwide rules and expectations of decorum and consequences for infractions of the rules. Most rules were arbitrary, and most consequences ended in suspension out of school, which contributed largely to the school's reputation as a "dropout academy."

When asked about their instructional responsibilities, there were blank stares from the administrative team. Thus, the first order of business was to clarify new expectations and the job descriptions of the administrative staff. This required redefining daily and long-term practices of interacting with students and staff on every level. Fortunately, they responded positively to the clarifications. He provided them with professional development on monitoring instruction, working with difficult teachers and parents, and maintaining an orderly environment.

The teachers returned to school to their first professional development session led by the principal. This session, designed in collaboration and with input from faculty members who were available during the summer, clarified the new communications expectations throughout the school and in classrooms. A draft of the agreed-upon priorities and rules for the school were presented, discussed, and defined:

Be On Time

Be Prepared

Be Attentive

Be Courteous to Others

Teachers agreed to obtain student support and input on how these rules and expectations were to look in each classroom. In addition they agreed that teachers would increase support through greater visibility in hallways and at doorways between classes.

The new principal then met with students by grade level during the first week of school to articulate how these expectations would elevate their school experiences. Students overwhelmingly responded positively. At the faculty meeting at the end of the first week, teachers were very pleased with the direction their school was going in, and they complimented their students and the administrative team for their positive efforts.

Another expectation from the principal was that all faculty meetings and departmental meeting were reinstated, and they should also be professional development opportunities. Each department was required to meet biweekly, and meetings were not to exceed one hour. In addition, there was a monthly faculty meeting that would also include professional development activities that were initially planned by the administrative team and teacher leaders (TLs). These meetings grew in popularity for their content and the snacks and food that were served.

Recognition and Rewards

Leaders who have developed a consistently visible means of public acknowledgments, recognition, and rewards for all stakeholders' achievements and contributions have captured a major way that people are proud to be a part of the school or district. This applies to school- and community-based stakeholders. It is a basic need of many to be recognized and rewarded for good performance. Recognizing superior performance publicly and providing open and honest feedback help the school and district grow and make progress toward exceeding standards and goals. Providing these types of support will help stakeholders grow and obtain their fullest potential and professional goals.

Recognizing superior performance publicly and providing open and honest feedback help the school and district grow and make progress toward exceeding standards and goals.

An example in another school included a large display on a bulletin board in the main faculty lounge that featured a bucket spilling large drops of compliments and how the school or classroom climates were impacted. Staff members simply selected a "drop," wrote another staff member's name and an acknowledgment, appreciation, or compliment, and then posted it on the display. This became so popular that the board was changed every grading quarter, and groups of drops of ten or more were framed and distributed to the honorees along with a certificate of appreciation from the principal.

In many schools recognition from one's peers goes a long way. In some schools principals begin faculty meetings by having teachers compliment a peer about a strategy that was shared with them, recognizing their willingness to assist one of their students, or just to say thank you for being a great role model for other teachers. As it relates to professional development in schools facilitated by faculty, an acknowledgment in the form of note cards, flowers, a gift certificate to their favorite eating place, or a coffee mug goes miles to securing a caring and collegial school climate. An expression of thank-you for a job well done cheers up anyone who then feels he or she appreciated.

> Investing time to learn something in your profession makes you RICH in KNOWLEDGE, if you are not then it will make you POOR in your PEFORMANCE.

> —Sivaprakash Sidhu

A significant component of collegial climates in schools is knowledge sharing among the staff to strengthen and improve all aspects of the culture. As schools continue to face an array of complex challenges, professional development is one of the most powerful ways to create and sustain ongoing and adaptable changes that are necessary for improvements. Unfortunately, in too many settings, it is too low on the priority scale to make the maximum difference possible in supporting the improvements and increasing student achievement.

Quite simply, professional development for school staffs is one of the most important investments that can be made to improve education in schools, districts, and systems. The returns on this investment hinges on the alignment of the professional development to school needs anchored in data, the quality of the professional development, and the reception of the professional development. Professional development is the strongest strategy schools, districts, and systems can use to ensure that educators continue to strengthen their practice and effectiveness throughout their careers by providing ongoing learning opportunities. This, in turn, is a very major boost to schoolwide collegial climates that feature positive morale and strong job satisfaction.

The Value of Coaching

Job-embedded professional development in schools is training and support for teachers that can impact their daily practices and procedures regarding student achievement (Darling-Hammond & McLaughlin, 2011). It can be designed for individuals or small and large groups and occurs during work hours. Frequently, it is anchored in the professional knowledge and experiences that exist within the school. One of the most powerful and effective jobs of embedded professional development is coaching.

Coaching is focused on the technical components of instruction. It provides ongoing and consistent follow-up through demonstrations, modeling, conversations, and observations. Generally it involves a coach who has expertise in a specific content area and who works with teachers on specific goals for improving their instructional skills and repertoire.

In addition, there is growing recognition and understanding that leadership coaching is also extremely valuable in ongoing school improvements. Leadership preparation course work and training have often not kept pace with the growing complexities or the actual demands and needs of "active-duty" leaders. Today's experienced and novice leaders benefit from coaching support that helps them improve their performance through individual assessment and guidance. It is important that this coaching be action oriented, growth and learning focused, confidential, and strategic and succession oriented.

There are several other types of effective job-embedded coaching that include lesson studies, action research, peer observations, and examining student work. From these types of coaching, leaders learn and benefit from sharing, collaboration, and relevancy. Leaders also benefit from multiple opportunities to learn with sufficient time, space, structures, and support.

Adult Learners

The research about job-embedded professional learning is anchored in the ways that adults learn. Designing professional development should allow the staff to anchor new knowledge on preexisting knowledge, see that the professional development fits in with daily school operations, and understand the relevancy to their work.

Leaders must be aware and knowledgeable about the differences among adult learners and how children, adolescents, and teens learn. Many of us have observed excellent practitioners who work extremely well with students only to "bomb out" when promoted to lead adults in schools.

Although many skills transfer from working with students to working with adults, there must be a significant recognition that adult learners require more opportunities for self-direction, clarity of purpose, rationales for changes, autonomous responsibilities, and relevancy of the work.

Understanding the distinctions between andragogy and pedagogy is critical.

SPOTLIGHT ON EFFECTIVE PRACTICE: PROFESSIONAL DEVELOPMENT

School leaders must be chief architects, advocates, and supporters of professional development. It's often helpful when they are also participants and sometimes facilitators. Using the achievement and other data from her students and faculty, a high school principal collaborated with several teacher leaders to design and implement an embedded schoolwide professional development model. This model was a yearlong program that began with using the master schedule as a tool for change.

The daily schedule was revised to support professional development participation by every teacher during the contracted day and to allow for designated TLs to consistently meet, study current research, and plan professional development sessions with the principal twice per week. This group of leaders practiced their delivery skills and follow-up classroom observation skills among each other prior to facilitating sessions with other faculty members. The results included achievement data that climbed from passing two of the Virginia Standards of Learning Tests to passing 9 of the 11 tests within the first year. In addition, 99 percent of the faculty requested additional professional development sessions on their survey. The teacher leaders were ecstatic!

Summary

The authors provided several examples of ways to embed professional development into school life with minimum budgetary costs. The most effective and sustainable professional development is that which is offered to stakeholders by colleagues. Another crucial component to boosting collegial climates is ensuring that current stakeholders are invested in identifying, choosing, and supporting their colleagues and new hires as much as possible. Several strategies that can help accomplish this were addressed.

Professional development activities are not exclusive to teachers but to support personnel as well. It is necessary to involve teacher aides, security personnel, secretaries, the school nurse, and maintenance staff in a variety of professional development activities. Their participation is important in their individual roles in supporting the instructional and safety issues of the school. Developing a schoolwide and districtwide professional development plans and implementing them is an essential component of increasing and improving student achievement. Creating the plan involves facilitating fearless conversations that examine less popular and less visible areas of schooling that need attention.

Reflections

The following questions are designed to provoke additional thinking and discussions about boosting collegial climates by providing embedded professional development.

1. What are the three most-needed professional development experiences for our school or district?

2. How are we ensuring that professional development is aligned with our mission, vision, identified needs, and goals?

3. How are we developing capacity for managing, delivering, and researching professional development among the faculty and staff?

4. What incentives and recognitions are offered or available to motivate, inspire, and encourage faculty and staff for improving, growing, and excelling?

Chapter 7

Planning for Success

> A goal without a plan is just a wish.
>
> —Antoine de Saint-Exupery

To make a difference in many school communities, strong dedication and commitment to improve are required from school leaders. It takes bold and fearless actions to ward off the saboteurs and naysayers who fear changes or who want to maintain the status quo. In the course of developing sound plans for school improvement, many school leaders need help in determining where and how to start their planning efforts to make overall improvements in teaching, instructional leadership, and/or organizational management.

Focused action planning is a skill set that can be developed and strengthened, and it is a critical part of making a positive difference as a vital component of effective leadership skills. Thus, it is critical to improving the school achievement opportunities for students, faculty, and staff and the school's community. We discussed creating and sustaining a viable learning and working environment, crafting and supporting a strong mission and vision, providing effective and user-friendly feedback, involving parents in the process, managing the school's culture, and providing professional development activities—all of which requires a well-designed plan. Every plan needs to begin with an end in mind and should be purposefully developed to get done what needs to get done for the benefit of students and the school community.

Planning With Data Teams

For school leaders, planning should start with using collected data to identify the learning needs of their students. Decisions have to be made that include determining what data are available and choosing which additional data need to be collected. It is generally best to identify faculty and parent stakeholders to work on a data team to analyze it, make decisions based upon what it reveals, set goals, and design plans to address those goals. Data team members also generally serve as leaders who support colleagues in implementing those plans. Selecting data team members is a process that requires careful attention. The data team should be a group whose members are identified based on the skills, talents, strengths, and knowledge each individual offers. Teams have to comprise individuals who understand and support the vision and mission of the school and who can and are willing to contribute based on their expertise, interests, and commitment.

Beware of common potential setbacks that include identifying well-meaning teachers who volunteer for tasks that they are not able or willing to sufficiently commit through to completion. Another pitfall can be choosing teachers who are popular but not particularly productive. A common mismatch occurs when leaders assign teachers who "need help" to the teams with the hopes that they will somehow become motivated to "get better." Team members, if possible, need to be people who are willing to work beyond the school day, able to work collaboratively and cooperatively with others, and who have the respect of their peers.

People who do this work are called upon to use a variety of skills: organizational skills for overseeing the coordination of multiple assessments; software skills for making the best use of technology; and people skills for interacting effectively with school staff and district personnel. Data team members need to have a clear understanding of effective teaching practices so that they know what kinds of charts, information, and templates teachers find most useful (Boudett, City, & Murnane, 2005).

Leaders need to understand that the collection and management of data can be a daunting task if assigned to one or two individuals. Thus, it is important for school leaders to develop data teams with individuals who have divergent points of view and who have the ability to appreciate input from others. A team should share the same sense of urgency for the school's overall improvement and see data collection and analysis as a means to move the school toward greater student achievement. And most important, leaders need to provide these team members with the resources (including time), training, and support needed to get their individual and collective tasks accomplished.

Once the team is trained and developed, appropriate roles must then be designated and, in some cases, reassigned. For example, a data team does not simply collect and analyze data; there must be discussions about what data need to be collected, who should collect it, and how they should report their findings to the entire team. During the initial meetings, the roles that should be assigned include the reporter, who will discuss the findings of the group; a recorder, who takes copious notes for distribution to the entire team; and a facilitator, who will lead the discussion around the data that have been shared. These roles should be rotated among the group, whenever feasible, to help ensure that all members fully participate and lead.

One of the first things that need to be done as the data team is developed is to collectively determine how when and where meetings will be conducted. Determining meeting norms will save everyone a lot of time and effort, and everyone will leave each meeting feeling that something was accomplished. A designated meeting space that includes the team's storage of materials, equipment, and other resources is also important. The following are a few suggested norms that can be considered for adoption:

- An agenda will be developed for every meeting and distributed to all members two days before the meeting takes place.

- Every meeting will begin and end at the specified time. Any agenda item not covered within that time will be placed at the top of the next meeting agenda.

- Every member will be on time for the meeting.

- Every team member will actively participate in these meetings so that the team can benefit from all points of view.

- Every team member will listen to and not talk over their colleagues.

- To the highest degree possible, the data team will strive to come to consensus on actions to be taken and recommendations to be made.

- At the end of some meetings, the roles of the facilitator, reporter, and recorder may be rotated.

Sharing the types of data collected and analyzed should always be done in a purposeful manner . . . Data teams and school leaders should recognize that their data need to tell a story.

Many school leaders conduct their first faculty meeting with a focus on the newly released state assessment data, thinking that the data presented will engage teachers in discussions about what they see. This is generally not an efficient or effective strategy.

Sharing the types of data collected and analyzed should always be done in a purposeful manner. Just throwing numbers on a screen does not generally support or encourage a meaningful discussion about the data. Data teams and school leaders should recognize that their data need to tell a story.

SPOTLIGHT ON EFFECTIVE PRACTICE: DATA, DATA, AND MORE DATA

In a high school in Virginia, one principal and his data team collected trend data over a period of four years in each core subject area and in the elective courses to show the areas of growth and areas of weakness. That led teachers to discuss what instructional strategies were used to create their gains and what strategies were needed to make improvements. This particular school, four years previously, had the lowest state achievement rates in this school district. One of the reasons for such low performance was that the previous teachers and staff members were not engaged in meaningful discussions about their data and did not provide the administrative support or insights to appropriately manage instruction.

When new leadership entered the school, they looked at more than achievement data. They examined data on student and staff attendance, suspensions, teacher disciplinary referrals, and parental involvement. This prompted the school leadership to design and implement a plan to effectively change these data. The plan was presented to stakeholders in draft form.

What the data revealed was that the daily student attendance of this school was less than 65 percent, students were suspended at an alarming rate for minor offenses, approximately 10 percent of the teachers wrote 100 percent of the referrals for minor infractions,

(Continued)

(Continued)

and to top it off there were little or no records of parental engagement or contacts initiated by staff in this school. When they examined the achievement data, they could see that a significant cause of poor test scores was partially due to overall student attendance and suspensions. The data team, with other school leaders, drilled down to student-by-student data that revealed more than 60 percent of the students in this school were reading below grade level.

A plan was revised and implemented to address the issues that the data revealed. The first step in the plan was to create and engage an instructional leadership team. That team included the principal, assistant principals, and department chairs and, from the district level, the assistant superintendent for instruction and the reading and math specialists. It later became known as the "A TEAM" (Academic Team). In its first meeting it was decided that they would meet with students, grade-level teams, parents, and community members as focus groups to discuss their findings and obtain input as to how to resolve the collective problems.

When meeting with the grade-level teams, the discussions centered on reading and student behaviors. Teachers felt strongly that reading was definitely a big problem, and they did not feel that they knew enough about reading to make an impact in their classroom instruction. Relating to student discipline, they felt that most of the students were well behaved when they were in class, but there were a few who constantly were disruptive, mainly because they were absent most of the time and, when they were in the classroom, they were unable to remain on task.

As a result of these meetings, the primary focus of the school became literacy improvement. The central office administration secured a grant that funded intensive literacy integration training that helped teachers learn to teach reading across the content areas. This training equipped teachers with a variety of reading strategies that they could implement to better engage struggling students.

To address the issues of discipline, the administrative team followed up with support for teachers using a variety of options. Connecting with and engaging parents resulted in significantly improving the attendance and behavioral problems.

According to the National Center for Educational Statistics (2012), it is important to note that at the state and district levels, engaging with local K–12 stakeholders is crucial to ensuring successful development and improving achievement. Involving multiple stakeholders helps identify, align, and leverage existing and new resources. Such involvement can also help develop tools and various support systems that will help reach the identified goals.

SPOTLIGHT ON EFFECTIVE PRACTICE: PLANNING FOR SUCCESS FOR ALL STUDENTS

When meeting with a focus group of students who were cutting classes, or being disruptive in class, they were very vocal in expressing their perspectives that in many of their classes, they felt the teachers didn't care if they passed or failed. They shared their perceptions that the teachers would lecture them every day with little or no student participation. They stated that it was easy to cut these classes, and in some cases, they believed teachers invited them to do so.

Later their parents had some interesting comments as well. These parents stated that the only time they heard from a teacher was when there was a problem, or they were not made aware that there was a problem until they heard from an administrator.

(Continued)

(Continued)

This meeting led to some fearless and courageous conversations with some teachers, individually, by the principal. It also prompted a conversation with the entire staff regarding classroom discipline beginning with high expectation and overall classroom management issues. It was made clear to the faculty that many disciplinary issues began and often could end at the classroom level.

One of the strategies that was employed to get this message across to all teachers was to have teachers who had successful classroom management practices conduct professional development for teachers who recognized that they were having difficulties in this area. A wonderful result was the type of collegial professional environment that was created by this practice. Teachers began to conduct peer observations and invite colleagues into their classrooms to give them some feedback when they tried different instructional strategies. Teachers also began to talk about students in positive ways rather than complaining about what was wrong with them; they began sharing more about the progress that was being made with hard-to-reach students.

This led to a more student-friendly environment, where the intent was to "nice them to death." The school staff was aligned with research findings that were later published in the *Journal of Applied Behavior Analysis* (Allday & Pakurar, 2007), which stated, "When teachers greeted students at the door, on-task behavior during the first ten minutes of class increased from a mean of 45% in baseline to a mean of 75%." The day began with more than 90 percent of the faculty and staff outside greeting students at the beginning of the day. In addition, all the teachers were outside their classrooms greeting students and ushering them on their way during class changes. At the end of the day, the faculty members were again at the busses sending students on their way home.

Planning for Student Engagement

Principals and other school leaders need to have a thorough understanding of instructional methodologies that help teachers engage a broader range of students at all times.

Planning for student engagement, an important activity, extends from the simplest level of greeting students as they enter the classroom to well-planned lessons that are relevant and actively engage them. Lessons must focus on the essential skills and information that students need to learn, apply, and/or think about. There must be ongoing discussions about the level of student engagement and how to plan accordingly. In addition to these discussions, school leaders need to plan professional development activities throughout the year on this singular topic.

Joshua Block (2013) cites that by using backwards design (McTighe and Wiggins, 2005), he determined six different engagement strategies that should be consistently used. He recommends planning for (1) authentic learning, (2) inquiry, (3) collaboration, (4) integrating the arts, (5) presentation and performance, and (6) integrating technology in each course. These six strategies are a sound basis for fearless conversations with and among teachers regarding improving student engagement. Authentic learning experiences allow students to experience and explore experiential learning.

In addition, Audrey Rule (2016) of the State University of New York at Oswego, cites the following four themes that support authentic learning:

1. Choose activities that involve real-world problems and that mimic the work of professionals—they should involve presentation of findings to audiences beyond the classroom.

2. Use open-ended inquiry, thinking skills, and metacognition.

3. Students engage in discourse and social learning in a community of learners.

4. Students direct their own learning in project work.

Leaders know that engaging students in collaborative learning experiences helps them learn to work in groups and understand that learning can be an interdependent activity where students learn from each other. However, leaders are not always knowledgeable about ways to make this happen. Several powerful strategies are anchored in collaborative learning strategies.

Collaborative learning is commonly illustrated when groups of students work together to search for understanding, meaning, or solutions or to create an artifact or product of their learning. Furthermore, collaborative learning redefines traditional student–teacher relationships in the classroom, which results in controversy over whether this paradigm is more beneficial than harmful. Collaborative learning activities can include collaborative writing, group projects, joint problem solving, debates, study teams, and other activities (Collaborative Learning, n.d.).

Integrating the arts in education allows students to use their creativity and abilities to express themselves in positive ways and demonstrate what they have learned. William Sloan (2009) points out that arts education advocates argue that whereas teaching art for art's sake is certainly beneficial for all students, studies show that participating in the arts can actually boost student achievement in other academic areas such as mathematics.

Have students make presentations and performances through project-based learning. This develops their speaking, thinking, and presentation skills.

Another effective planning protocol is having students make presentations and performances through project-based learning. This protocol further develops their speaking, thinking, and presentation skills that are necessary for the 21st-century workplace. Project-based learning is another student-centered pedagogy that involves a dynamic classroom approach in which student acquire a deeper knowledge through active exploration of real-world challenges and problems.

School leaders need to model the use of and be knowledgeable about integrating technology in their schools. Today's students live in a technological age, and as educators we must learn to engage them using tools from a world in which they are most familiar. Planning the integration of technology throughout instruction is essential.

Planning for Parental Participation

SPOTLIGHT ON EFFECTIVE PRACTICE: PROVIDE LEADERSHIP OPPORTUNITIES FOR PARENTS TOO

Although we dedicated Chapter 4 to exploring effective parent partnerships, to include and involve community stakeholders, planning is essential.

A parent–teacher organization did not exist in a particular high school for several years. To begin to address this concern, the school administrators invited all parents to attend a potluck dinner where all could bring a dish of their choosing to share. Something about sharing food can bring people together, and this eventually resulted in the identification and creation of a very active parent–teacher organization in this school.

After the meal, school achievement and performance data were shared with the parents, and discussions about what they could do to help with the issues that faced the school followed. Parents stated that they were not invited into the school in the past, and even though they were concerned about the progress and achievement of their children, they were not sure how to collectively address those concerns.

This school leadership built a coalition of parents, faculty, and student collaborators. The plan to include parents more in the

(Continued)

(Continued)

planning was working by bringing all stakeholders together and obtaining more ideas and commitments to help improve the daily life of this school. "Keeping Students First in All Endeavors" became the motto for the school as the parent–teacher organization grew larger and more involved.

To address the student attendance issues that plagued this school, particularly in the first semester, another plan was designed and implemented. This plan began with every teacher making contact with every parent or guardian of those students who were chronically absent or late to classes. After teachers made this contact and talked to parents about the importance of their children being in school and on time every day, the school immediately began to see some progress.

For students who continued to be late or absent, a call from the students' counselor took place, and they discussed in detail the number of credits that these students needed to graduate and the progress of each child toward completing requirements to graduate with his or her class. Many students who were overage had the option of taking a GED prep course or to prepare themselves to complete their high school graduation requirements by enrolling into a custom designed laboratory, where students were able to complete their requirements using a computer-based learning system. To teach these children, they had to physically be in school, and parental support was essential to making improvements regarding this goal.

Within a year this school began to see exponential growth in their achievement based on the planning efforts that were put in place. Attendance increased from a daily rate of 65 percent to 93 percent. The number of teacher disciplinary referrals was minimal, and the levels of parental involvement increased significantly. The number of suspensions was in single digits each semester. Additionally, students began to take pride in themselves and in their school. The principal and teachers took every opportunity to celebrate their successes. During the third year of implementing these plans, the school achieved full state accreditation.

Planning for Communication

One of the most important activities that principal leaders need to engage in is ensuring that communications to teachers, students, and the community remain consistently static free. A monthly newsletter published electronically and on paper the first day of each month, providing updates on the life of the school, helps keep everyone informed. This should include current data on local and state assessments and a schedule of events for the current month that includes times for tutorial and enrichment activities. All members of the school community, students, parents, community organizations, and teachers should be invited to contribute to the newsletter by posting announcements, notices, and congratulatory notes to teachers, staff, or students.

In addition, plan a monthly Have Coffee With the Principal session to be conducted every first Monday of the month. This activity can be open to parents, teachers, and community members who would like face time with the principal to discuss their concerns or just have a good conversation and a warm cup of coffee. Some principal leaders feature quarterly chats with the principal for faculty members to attend, have a snack, and share issues and concerns. Information, ideas, and input from these chats can be included in improvement planning processes. These sessions can become very popular when faculty recognize their contributions among the plans and changes that occur in the school. They are worth the time investment.

Planning Tools

One of the more powerful planning tools in the educational arena is the Daggett system for Effective Instruction, which includes specific guiding protocols to help leaders start planning effectively for schools and school district improvements (Daggett, 2015). Using this readiness rubric, schools have to do some deep needs assessments by asking several key questions. These questions include: What is the vision for each school? What are the core values of teachers, as school faculty members? What are the stated and unstated goals? How will these goals be achieved? What is the desired service for students, and who will they become upon graduation? What is believed about student academic achievement and achievement in other areas? Responses to these questions are the foundation for designing a good plan to address concerns and issues in schools and school districts (see Appendix 1).

Another tool that leaders can consider using for effective school and district planning is the process that is recommended by the School Improvement Network (2015). This process includes five steps: (1) start with a vision, (2) conduct a needs assessment, (3) identify goals and objectives, (4) outline specific action steps, and (5) involve all stakeholders in the process. We recommend a sixth step that would be: review and revise.

One of the planning tools that was used successfully by one of the authors to help keep everyone in perpetual motion toward improvements to gain full accreditation listed the goals and objectives, person(s) responsible, timeline for completion, and budget. Each committee, subcommittee, and focus group used the same template to articulate, organize, and help accomplish their goals (see Table 7.1).

One of the pitfalls that school leaders must avoid is to assume that teachers fully understand the difference between goals and objectives. Thus, it is generally helpful to ensure that they know the rationale for setting goals and objectives and how these goals

Table 7.1 Planning Tool

Goal:		
Objective:		
Action Steps: 1. 2. 3. 4.		
Person(s) Responsible:		
Budget		
Materials	Supplies	Other
Timeline:		
Initiated	Completed	Comments

and objectives help steer schools toward more productive futures. Leaders must clearly communicate to all members of the school community that goal setting is a necessary activity to move the school forward.

SPOTLIGHT ON EFFECTIVE PRACTICE: GOALS AND OBJECTIVES

At Exemplary High School, it was very important to clarify for everyone how goals without objectives are rarely accomplished, whereas objectives without goals will not move the school in a more successful direction. The two concepts are separate but closely related. Goals are long-term aims that are desired. Objectives are concrete attainments that can be achieved by following a certain number of steps. Goals and objectives are often used interchangeably, but the main differences are revealed in their level of concreteness. Objectives are very concrete, whereas goals are less structured (Difference Between Goals and Objectives, n.d.).

Based on the planning efforts and use of data, in the second year of its opening, this high school's improvement focus included mathematics as well as literacy. The master schedule, a powerful tool and frequently underutilized, was redesigned to allow teachers to have common planning time where they met in interdisciplinary groups to discuss individual student needs.

Also, through the planning efforts of both students and teachers, a student–teacher mentor program was developed in which 15 students were assigned to every teacher to ensure that every student was well known and perhaps had a positive relationship with at least one adult in the building. Time was built into the schedule for these teachers to meet with their mentees on a regular basis.

Lesson plans were developed for the sessions that addressed several topics that included but were not limited to Internet use, safety and security issues, death and dying, family life, and so on. In addition, students developed a peer mediation program in which disputes between and among students were resolved by students.

Planning Goals and Objectives

Using data leads to focused planning at multiple levels to incorporate various activities that address what the data reveals. Success requires planning. Arthur Ashe once said, "Success is a journey, not a destination. The doing is often more important than the outcome." What is it that school leaders must do to get the results they want? More specifically, what is it that school leaders must plan to obtain the results they want? Among the various responsibilities of leaders one of the most important tasks is planning the day and organizing time on a daily basis. As teachers are expected to have daily plans, it is necessary for school leaders to also have daily plans.

> *Just as teachers need to be visibly involved with students to maximize their learning, leaders need to be visibly involved in instruction to ensure improvements.*

As a part of daily planning, principals and other school administrators should be visible throughout the day in classrooms as well as other areas of the school. Although unscheduled issues, disruptions, and many other concerns will occur that require immediate attention, these leaders must plan appropriately for their primary focus to remain on instruction within the building. Just as teachers need to be visibly involved with students to maximize their learning, leaders need to be visibly involved in instruction to ensure improvements. It is essential to schedule classroom visits and provide feedback (not just commentary) to those visited in formal and informal ways. It is also crucial for principals to regularly meet with other building leaders in a consistent manner and ensure that those times are uninterrupted unless there's an emergency.

The 80–20 strategy mentioned earlier then becomes more manageable when the emphasis is 80 percent of time spent on instruction and 20 percent of time spent on management. Whereas instruction should drive the school, good management ensures that support is in place to facilitate good instruction. The management ensures that the facilities are conducive to learning, sufficient supplies and equipment are available, and the support staff remain focused on their contributions to the learning environment.

Various tools should be fully utilized to organize time and promote and share positive news and information to the community. For example, one of the best organizing tools a principal can use is a tickler file, which can be kept on a cell phone, a tablet, or another device, that includes all of the important events, critical activities, memos, and time deadlines (end of semester or quarter, testing, grading periods, open house, parent conferences, etc.) for each month.

Principal's Daily Planning Guide

For many years leaders have struggled with planning their daily routines, but current electronic devices allow us to keep vital schedules and information with us at all times. Keeping in mind the 80–20 rule, the form in Table 7.2 can be used to guide daily activities. This format is user-friendly to help prioritize tasks and to remember the tasks that need to be accomplished. This planning guide can be installed on electronic devices and help one see at a glance the balance or lack of balance between instructional leadership tasks and management tasks.

One of our weaker areas as educators is consistently building in evaluations of our practices and processes. Too frequently, we make powerful plans but do not have formative ways to assess their effectiveness. This part of planning is critically important. Good ongoing assessments, benchmarks, and summative evaluations are important products of thoughtful planning.

Leaders should develop or strengthen the ability to ask good questions and increase skills in understanding about how to find valid answers—the refinement of everyday thinking. Effective and timely benchmark examinations and evaluations provide information that is sound, meaningful, and sufficiently reliable to use in making thoughtful and responsible decisions

Table 7.2 Daily Planning Guide

| School Name: _____ Principal _____ | | |
| Week of _____ | | |
Date	**Instructional Tasks**	**Managerial Tasks**
Monday	1. 2. 3. 4.	1. 2. 3. 4.
Tuesday	1. 2. 3. 4.	1. 2. 3. 4.
Wednesday	1. 2. 3. 4.	1. 2. 3. 4.
Thursday	1. 2. 3. 4.	1. 2. 3. 4.
Friday	1. 2. 3. 4.	1. 2. 3. 4.

about professional development processes and effects (Guskey, 2002). It is important to monitor the progress of school and district planning goals.

For example, several schools staffs have goals of creating smaller school communities within their buildings, but school leaders sometimes begin the planning of these communities without having a viable guide to assist them. To establish viable guidelines, school leaders will need to be clear about the rationale for this strategy, organize specific tasks, assign the tasks to appropriate stakeholders, and monitor the progress of all activities that will help them reach the goal of creating small communities.

An example is how a high school in Georgia and one in Connecticut developed their smaller learning communities by creating academies. In these schools, the academies that were appropriate for their communities and student populations were engineering, technology, and construction; visual and performing arts; consumer, health, and political science; and a freshman academy.

The engineering academy offered college preparation classes with an engineering career-related focus. This program connected themed academic courses with engineering electives. Students took courses related to engineering, technology, and construction. The visual and performing arts academy offered college preparation classes with a performing career-related focus. These programs connected themed academic courses with visual and performing arts. Students took courses related to music, theater, art, audiovisual skills, technology, and communications. The consumer, health, and political science academy offered college preparation classes with a health- and/or politics-related career focus. These programs connected themed academic courses with public service–based electives. Students took courses in the consumer, health, and political science areas. The freshman academy's focus was on promotion of freshman students into one of the career academies through providing them with foundational classes that assisted them in choosing a career pathway toward graduation and entry into the world of work, higher education, or the military. The result of these academies was a rigorous, relevant, real-world education for the students.

Summary

Leaders benefit from having a flexible plan that can be adjusted and revised as progress is made. A good plan provides leaders with concrete actionable strategies that are unlike a rocking chair, which generates a lot of motion but doesn't go anywhere. An effective plan has built-in accountability and ongoing capacity building to address change and achievement. Effective planning is proactive and strengthens the school's culture while helping reinforce relationships and a sense of community.

Reflections

The following questions are designed to provoke additional thinking and discussions about planning for success.

1. What are the indicators that demonstrate a sense of urgency among the school's and district's leadership to plan for the success of all students? What are the data upon which the planning is based?

2. What skills do I personally need to improve and model to become a stronger leader of learning in our school/district?

3. Where are the resources that will help increase planning leadership skills?

Conclusion

In this conclusion we'd like to highlight some of the key points in the book as well as offer advice and ideas on getting started and share an adjustable operational template, checklists, and other tools for planning. We encourage you to use the templates in the book to guide planning processes to strengthen your leadership to improve student achievement.

Overall we encourage all school leaders to remember that school community stakeholders take their cues from you. They watch, listen, and follow your leadership. They care what you think about and will think and act on what you care about. We, the authors, recognize that there is an unlimited wealth of information, experiences, and ideas that are relevant to sound and effective leadership. We wanted to openly and honestly address some of the common dysfunctions that limit progress within typical school and school system leadership that few people are comfortable discussing.

> *Remember that school community stakeholders take their cues from you. They watch, listen, and follow your leadership. They care what you think about and will think and act on what you care about.*

This book has hopefully provided some new, validated, timely, and relevant ideas for aspiring, newly hired, and experienced school and/or school system leaders. The contents, of course, do not address all contingencies but perhaps jump-start some additional thinking about chronic issues and shed some additional light on upcoming issues that typically accompany change and growth. The book is a salient effort to create another leadership pathway on the journey toward success that ultimately benefits kids.

Chapter 1 examines the critical importance of creating and sustaining a work environment that allows and supports growth, is focused on how to facilitate that growth, and points out some mistakes to avoid. An important reminder is that antiquated traditions, political expediency, and fear of making mistakes will often interfere with the overall responsibility of many leaders to lead. Effective leaders continually practice and refine skills required to step up to the plate and apply their best insights and experiences to make progress.

Chapter 2 reminds us that if we don't know where we're going, that's exactly where we'll arrive. Ensuring that we have clear visions and missions and ensuring that our stakeholders also own them are major keys to effecting change and promoting growth and improvements. Therefore, it's in our best interests to define our directions and make sure that all are prepared for the journey.

Chapter 3 reminds us that through honesty, there is greater clarity. If we want to support our stakeholders on their journeys, leaders must wear coaching, teaching, motivational, and inspirational hats. These hats must be worn at the right times for the right reasons and in the right ways. This requires leaders to share honest, useful, and effective feedback to stakeholders.

Chapter 4 includes perspectives on working with an often highly valuable group of stakeholders—parents and community members. Frequently in our zeal as leaders, we can become so immersed in our goals and work to provide the best educational experiences possible that we neglect to include this group of stakeholders in ways that maximizes their involvement in this process. They can then become underutilized resources.

Chapter 5 recognizes the accuracy of a quote from an unknown source: "Change is inevitable unless it is from a vending machine." Leading a perpetually changing school and/or school system will frequently yield the greater benefits to the stakeholders when a deep understanding of defining, building, and sustaining the culture of the organization is understood, valued, and articulated by everyone involved. It reminds us of the significance of the old saying about progress in that it is more powerful when "we are singing from the same sheet of music."

Chapter 6 speaks to the essential but often overlooked necessity of job-embedded growth and improvement opportunities. Educators often acknowledge that time is a commodity that is too often in short supply. Leaders can often increase the efficiency of what we making more creative use of the time available. This will often allow us to actually differentiate professional development opportunities to meet a broader range of needs. Schedules and routines that rarely change to incorporate growth options for the faculty and staff are underutilized resources.

Chapter 7 is a critical chapter in that boosting organizational skills and strengths through more effective planning and communications does increase productivity and options for success. Specific planning for success increases the chances that success will actually occur. Even when mistakes are made as we sometimes try to fix symptoms rather than the real problems, it is still better to have a plan as plans can change, but without one, continued floundering is the usual result.

We invite readers to contribute their stories, ideas, errors to avoid, and successful strategies with us. Doing so may help make all of us stronger and allow us to continue to grow and learn from each other in relevant and meaningful ways. As there are numerous additional important aspects of effective leadership to address, this book is a beginning and addresses a few of those areas that confront leaders on a daily and consistent basis. Sharing your information will constitute permission for us to utilize it in future work to help other leaders. Names, locations, and identities may be changed to ensure anonymity.

Appendices

Appendix A

Daggett System for Effective Instruction Questionnaire

Please complete the following readiness rubric as a team to effectively understand where your school or district is in terms of readiness to *effectively* act as a *system to improve instruction.*

It is important to first complete this rubric as a team and then move to creating action plans based on the three segments of the Daggett System of Effective Instruction (DSEI). The action plans are provided and should be completed collaboratively based on the highest-need practice areas for each of the segments.

If you need to refer to the DSEI white paper or element descriptors, you may access them at DSEI white paper (www.leadered.com/our-philosophy/dsei/questionnaire).

KEY: Best Practices Descriptors

1. ***Firmly Established:*** The practice is long-standing, is deeply embedded in the district or school culture, and is embraced as a priority by all stakeholders.

2. ***Partially Established:*** The practice is in the beginning stages of implementation, and there is significant support for the practice among many stakeholders. However, the practice is not equally understood or valued among all groups. The practice is not implemented with fidelity across the system.

3. ***In Planning Stages:*** There is significant support for the practice across the system. It is seen as a high priority by many, and planning is underway to implement and/or pilot it.

4. ***Not Evident:*** The practice is not viewed as a high priority by many stakeholders, and there is no evidence of planning or implementation.

Organizational Leadership Questionnaire

Reflect on the following questions, and identify the level of readiness for each item.

OL3: Which statement best describes your school's implementation of vision-related goals?				
❑ Not Yet Started	❑ Beginning	❑ Emerging	❑ Developed	❑ Well Developed
There has been no discussion to articulate a vision nor any attempt to realize one.	It is understood that without structures and systems in place to support vision implementation, a vision alone has no use.	Key stakeholders have developed a timeline to put strategic systems and structures into place to realize the vision.	Difficult conversations have occurred around parting with outdated systems and structures that do not serve the vision.	All new, possible systems and structures are routinely vetted against the vision, and only tools that support vision over time are utilized.
Evidence to support rating:				

OL4: Which statement best describes your school's perceptions and treatment of leadership?

❑ Not Yet Started	❑ Beginning	❑ Emerging	❑ Developed	❑ Well Developed
Control is centralized in the leadership team.	It is understood that too much control is centralized within the leadership team.	There is a general belief that leadership is a disposition, not a position, and something that is most effective when shared.	Leadership is actively encouraged at all levels.	There is a concerted effort to support leaders and always aim to spot and nurture new leadership talent.

Evidence to support rating:

OL5: Which statement best describes your school's current approach to teacher support and evaluation?

❑ Not Yet Started	❑ Beginning	❑ Emerging	❑ Developed	❑ Well Developed
Standards and protocol overwhelm any efforts to take control of the teacher evaluation system.	It is known that staff perceives teacher evaluations as punitive, demoralizing, and leaving too many teachers without support.	Difficult conversations around evaluations have occurred, and a commitment to making changes and aligning evaluations to overall vision and goals has been made.	Collaboration with staff to determine what they need to feel supported in achieving professional success has taken place.	The professional development and staff support system is regularly evaluated for efficacy, and improvements are made as needed.

Evidence to support rating:

OL6: Which statement best describes your school's views and use of data?				
❑ Not Yet Started	❑ Beginning	❑ Emerging	❑ Developed	❑ Well Developed
There has been no discussion about using data to track the efficacy and progress of programs and initiatives.	It is known that data can provide Important information around the progress toward meeting goals and the efficacy of programs and initiatives.	Data systems have been strategically vetted and selected to fit the district-specific vision and goals.	Data systems are routinely audited to ensure they continue to align to vision and goals.	Broad and varied data are regularly collected, and data results and analysis are communicated transparently to support strategic decision-making.
Evidence to support rating:				

Source: International Center for Leadership in Education. Reprinted with permission.

Instructional Leadership Questionnaire

Reflect on the following questions, and identify the level of readiness for each item.

IL1: Which statement best describes the views your school has on the need for change and improvement?				
❑ Not Yet Started	❑ Beginning	❑ Emerging	❑ Developed	❑ Well Developed
There is no need for change and improvement in our school(s).	Data and evidence have been used to support and express a need for change and improvement in our school.	New data is routinely gathered to reinforce and communicate the need for change and improvements in our school.	Formal discussion forums have been held to ensure stakeholders are involved in planning necessary changes and improvements.	There is an established program of frequent discussion, varied in format and approach, to assess school-wide fidelity and progress in making improvements and changes.
Evidence to support rating:				

IL2: Which statement best describes the views of your school about aligning curriculum and assessments to standards?

❏ Not Yet Started	❏ Beginning	❏ Emerging	❏ Developed	❏ Well Developed
The need for curriculum and assessments to be aligned to standards is not discussed.	It is known that curriculum and assessments must all be aligned to standards.	It is recognized that instruction must be differentiated so that all students can demonstrate mastery of standards.	The efficacy of Instructional strategies used to ensure all students demonstrate mastery of standards is regularly tracked and monitored.	An interdisciplinary curriculum that aligns vision, standards, and curriculum and empowers teachers to collaborate and innovate has been implemented.

Evidence to support rating:

IL3: Which statement best describes the views your school has on literacy, math, and technology integration?

❏ Not Yet Started	❏ Beginning	❏ Emerging	❏ Developed	❏ Well Developed
There is no particular view of literacy, math, and technology integration.	It is known and believed that literacy, math, and technology must be integrated across disciplines if students are to be college and career ready.	There is a proactive effort to look for opportunities to maximize literacy, math, and technology integration across disciplines and communicate all ideas and plans with staff.	There is a schoolwide mind-set that we all must integrate literacy, math, and technology into all disciplines wherever appropriate and possible.	A formal and systematic approach to interdisciplinary integration of literacy, math, and technology is being implemented and overseen.

Evidence to support rating:

IL4: Which statement best describes the views your school has on using data to inform instruction?

❏ Not Yet Started	❏ Beginning	❏ Emerging	❏ Developed	❏ Well Developed
Data are not used to make instructional decisions.	It is known that using data allows for more sound instructional decisions.	There is a plan in place to collect varied data about student work to guide instructional decisions.	A collaborative decision-making model based on data and student performance with corresponding maps to guide instructional planning and contingencies has been developed.	As part of frequent conversations around student data, teachers are empowered to turn data into actionable instruction and intervention plans.

Evidence to support rating:

IL5: Which statement best describes the approach your school has to professional development for teachers?

❏ Not Yet Started	❏ Beginning	❏ Emerging	❏ Developed	❏ Well Developed
There is a professional development plan in place for teachers.	It is known that teachers must be supported in instructional mastery through professional development and learning opportunities.	Data play a key role in planning targeted professional development opportunities for teachers.	A formal and data-driven professional development program for teachers has been established.	The professional development program and its impact on instructional mastery for all teachers is routinely monitored for efficacy.

Evidence to support rating:

IL6: Which statement best describes the views of your school on family and community engagement?				
❑ Not Yet Started	❑ Beginning	❑ Emerging	❑ Developed	❑ Well Developed
There is no plan to engage families and the community in our school(s).	Basic school information is shared with families and the community.	It is routinely communicated to staff, families, and community that each plays a critical role in student achievement, and their involvement is encouraged.	Multiple strategic and convenient ways for families and the community to engage meaningfully in the student learning process are offered.	Protocols to monitor the quality and efficacy of family and community engagement initiatives are in place.
Evidence to support rating:				

Source: International Center for Leadership in Education. Reprinted with permission.

Teaching Questionnaire

Reflect on the following questions and identify the level of readiness for each item.

T1: Which statement best describes your school's approach to ensuring rigorous and relevant instruction?				
❑ Not Yet Started	❑ Beginning	❑ Emerging	❑ Developed	❑ Well Developed
There is no plan to ensure rigorous and relevant instruction.	There is awareness that classroom visits are the most effective tool to identify levels of rigor and relevance in each classroom.	There is a clearly communicated classroom visit plan in place and rubrics to guide evaluation and feedback.	Classrooms are routinely visited, and rubrics are used to guide productive, nonpunitive feedback sessions with teachers and discuss new ways to increase rigor and relevance for all students.	Teachers are regularly empowered to evaluate their own instruction against rigorous and relevant learning goals.
Evidence to support rating:				

T2: Which statement best describes the views and plans of your school to ensure that learner environments are engaging?

❑ Not Yet Started	❑ Beginning	❑ Emerging	❑ Developed	❑ Well Developed
There is no plan to ensure learner environments are engaging.	It is known that for learner environments to be engaging, they must be relationship based and aligned to student needs.	It is known that student insights are key to understanding the state of learning environments, and protocols have been put in place to make students feel safe and comfortable providing input, feedback, and reflection.	Leaders and teachers collaborate to interpret student feedback and use it to improve learner environments and enhance student-teacher relationships.	Staff is encouraged to share insights about and from students, so all staff can make more informed learner environment and student relationship-building decisions.

Evidence to support rating:

T3: Which statement best describes the views and plans your school has to support teacher content knowledge development?

❑ Not Yet Started	❑ Beginning	❑ Emerging	❑ Developed	❑ Well Developed
There is no plan to ensure teachers are always improving content area knowledge.	It is known that a plan is needed to support ongoing teacher content knowledge development.	An ongoing program to provide professional content knowledge learning, with a particular emphasis on training teachers to flexibly apply content to a range of topics, has been devised.	Professional content learning provides teachers with tools to flexibly and frequently apply content to college and career skills.	Teachers are consistently provided targeted feedback on their content learning progress toward expertise and flexible application to relevant learning for all students.

Evidence to support rating:

T4: Which statement best describes the relationship your school has with current learner research and technologies?

❑ Not Yet Started	❑ Beginning	❑ Emerging	❑ Developed	❑ Well Developed
Learner research and current technologies are not followed.	It is known that today's students learn differently and engage with technology uniquely, and instructional strategies must be selected with this in mind.	The latest learning research and current technologies are shared between and among teachers.	Collaboration is facilitated to find ways to integrate research-based best and next practices and current technologies into instruction wherever possible to ensure that instruction resonates with learners.	A formal and regularly monitored plan is in place to ensure research-based instructional strategies and current technologies are routinely and effectively used in all classrooms.

Evidence to support rating:

T5: Which statement best describes the approach your school has to student assessment data and instructional planning?

❑ Not Yet Started	❑ Beginning	❑ Emerging	❑ Developed	❑ Well Developed
There is no plan for using student assessment data to guide instructional planning.	It is understood that formative assessment tools can be powerful guides in day-to-day and week-to-week instructional planning.	Proactive collaboration time with teachers is used to select appropriate formative assessment tools that enable the most goal-aligned collection of data to help teachers plan instruction.	Meetings with students and teachers to help students understand that data are meant to support their learning paths to success are held.	Through regular dialogue, teachers are guided through the process of making independent decisions around how to use assessment data for preventative, not remedial, learning strategies.

Evidence to support rating:

T6: Which statement best describes the views and approach your school has to ongoing teacher professional development learning, and support?				
❏ Not Yet Started	❏ Beginning	❏ Emerging	❏ Developed	❏ Well Developed
There is no plan to support teacher development in an ongoing way.	It is openly acknowledged that teachers today are overwhelmed and need support.	Teacher input is valued in building a professional learning program that will provide teachers the support and tools they need to realize student achievement goals.	The development of personal learning networks is facilitated and encourages teachers to share resources and ideas and offer respectful feedback and support to each other.	Relevant strategies and tactics are routinely used to ensure teachers adopt a mind-set of continual improvement and feel safe and supported in asking for help.
Evidence to support rating:				

Source: International Center for Leadership in Education. Reprinted with permission.

Reference

Daggett, B. (2017). *Daggett System for Effective Instruction (DSEI) Questionnaire.* New York, NY: International Center for Leadership in Education. Retrieved from www.leadered.com/our-philosophy/dsei/questionnaire

Appendix B

An Invitation to Our Readers

One of the challenges of improving as leaders is to disrupt our isolation from major sources of power—each other. We invite you to share your experiences, thoughts, stories, ideas, and problems to help us create a powerful volume of resourceful tools that can benefit others. Our follow-up plan includes sharing information from our readers in a manner that may provide support to them and others. Please use the following guidelines:

School Name:	Your Name/Position:
School/District:	State:
1. Please limit your submission to two (2) pages or less.	
2. Please describe the pertinent demographics of your school or school district.	
3. Describe how sharing this information, problem, situation, and so on may benefit others.	
4. Submit your information electronically to ijones.depd@gmail.com or verajblake@gmail.com	
Submitting your ideas, stories, and so on constitute your giving permission for them to be used in future volumes. If your information is selected for inclusion in future sharing, names, school districts, and other identifiable information will be deleted and/or changed to preserve anonymity. Contributors will be acknowledged in the resource section of the book.	

References

Albemarle County Public Schools. (n.d.). Learning walks overview. Retrieved from https://www2.k12albemarle.org/acps/staff/tpa/documents/learning_walks_overview.pdf

Allday, R. A., & Pakurar, K. (2007). Effects of teacher greetings on student on-task behavior. *Journal of Applied Behavior Analysis, 40*(2), pp. 317–320. doi:10.1901/jaba.2007.86–06

Angelica, E. W. (2002). The Wilder nonprofit field guide to crafting effective mission and vision statements. Retrieved from http://www.volunteer-delaware.org/servlet/servlet.FileDownload?file=015A00000034wp1

Blanchard, K. & Bowles, S. (1997). *Gung ho.* New York, NY: William Morrow.

Block, J. (2013, October 1). Planning for engagement: 6 strategies for the year. *George Lucas Educational Foundation.* Edutopia. Retrieved from https://www.edutopia.org/blog/planning-for-engagement-6-strategies-joshua-block

Bosher, M., & Hazlewood, P. (2008). *Leading the leaders for the future: A transformational opportunity.* New York, NY: Continuum International Publishing Group.

Boudett, K. P., City, E. A., & Murnane, R. J. (2005). *Data wise: A step-by-step guide to using assessment results to improve teaching and learning.* Cambridge, MA: Harvard Education Press.

City, E. A, Elmore, R. F., Fiarman, S. E., & Teitel, L. (2009). *Instructional rounds in education.* Cambridge, MA: Harvard Education Press.

Clift, R.T., Houston, W. R., & Pugach, M. C. (1990). *Encouraging reflective practices in education: An analysis of issues and programs.* New York, NY: Teachers College Press.

Collaborative learning. (n.d.). In *Wikipedia.* Retrieved from https://en.wikipedia.org/wiki/Collaborative_learning

Daggett, W. (2015). The Daggett system for effective instruction. The International Center for Leadership in Education. Retrieved from http://www.leadered.com/pdf/daggett_system_for_effective_instruction_2014.pdf

Darling-Hammond, L., & McLaughlin, M. W. (2011, April). Policies that support professional development in an era of reform. *Phi Delta Kappan, 76*(8). Retrieved from http://journals.sagepub.com/doi/abs/10.1177/003172171109200622

Differences Between Goals and Objectives. (n.d.). *DifferenceBetween.net.* Retrieved from http://www.differencebetween.net/business/difference-between-goals-and-objectives

Egan, J. (n.d.) Goal setting. Retrieved from https://www.goalsforall.com/goal-setting.html

Gabriel, J., & Farmer, P.C. (2009). *How to help your school thrive without breaking the bank.* Alexandria, VA: ASCD Publications.

Great Schools Partnership. (2013). *The glossary of education reform.* Creative Commons Attribution-NonCommercial-ShareAlike 4.0 International License.

Guild, J. (2012). Learning walks: "Instructional rounds" for your school. *Independent School Magazine* (Winter 2012), 9.

Guskey, T. R. (2002). Does it make a difference? Evaluating professional development. *Educational Leadership, 59*(6), pp. 45–51.

Hattie, J. (2009). *Visible learning: A synthesis of over 800 meta-analyses related to achievement.* New York, NY: Routledge.

Marzano, R. (2003). *What works in schools: Translating research into action.* Alexandria, VA: Association for Supervision and Curriculum Development.

McNulty, R. (2016). *Changing school culture to truly reflect college and career.* Proceedings from the Model Schools Conference, Orlando, Florida.

McTighe, J, & Wiggins, G. (2005). *Understanding by design* (2nd ed.) Alexandria, VA: Association for Supervision and Curriculum Development.

National Center for Educational Statistics. (2012). *SLDS spotlight: State approaches to engaging local K–12 stakeholders.* Washington, DC: Author.

OnStrategy. (n.d.). *Overview of the strategic planning process* [Video]. Retrieved from http://www.m3planning.com

Tarrozi, G. (2003). Proceedings from the *NASSP Annual National Convention,* San Diego, CA.

Tomlinson, C. (1995). *How to differentiate instruction in mixed-ability classrooms.* Alexandria, VA: Association for Supervision & Curriculum Development.

Reeves, D. (2008). Leading to change/effective grading practices. *Educational Leadership, 65*(5), pp. 85–87.

Richmond City Public Schools. (n.d.). Mission. Retrieved from https://www.rvaschools.net/domain/6

Rule, A. (2016, August). The four characteristics of authentic learning. *Journal of Authentic Learning, 3*(1), pp. 1–10.

Saphier, J., & Gower, R. (1997). *The skillful teacher: Building your teacher skills* (5th ed.). Research for Better Teaching. Acton, MA: ASCD.

Sarason, S. B. (2002). *Educational reform: A self-scrutinizing memoir.* New York, NY: Teachers College Press.

Schlechty, P. (2011). *Engaging students: The next level of working on the work.* San Francisco, CA: Josey-Bass.

School Improvement Network. (2015). Four keys to successful school improvement. Retrieved from http://edivate.schoolimprovement.com/four-keys-to-successful-school-improvement

Sloan, W. (2009). Making content connections through arts integration. *Education Update,* 51(3). Retrieved from http://www.ascd.org/publications/newsletters/education-update/mar09/v0151/num03/Making-Content-Connections-Through-Arts-Integration.aspx

U.S. Department of Education. (1998). *The conditions of education 1998* (NCES 98–013). Washington DC: National Center for Educational Statistics.

Wiggins, G. (2012). Seven keys to effective feedback. *Educational Leadership, 70*(1), pp. 10–16.

Wormeli, R. (2006). *Fair isn't always equal: Assessing & grading in the differentiated classroom.* Portland: ME: Stenhouse Publishers.

Index

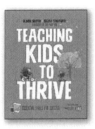

Leadership
that Makes
an Impact

Charlotte Danielson
Harness the power of informal professional conversation and invite teachers to boost achievement.

Liz Wiseman, Lois Allen, & Elise Foster
Use leadership to bring out the best in others—liberating staff to excel and doubling your team's effectiveness.

Eric Sheninger
Use digital resources to create a new school culture, increase engagement, and facilitate real-time PD.

Russell J. Quaglia, Michael J. Corso, & Lisa L. Lande
Listen to your school's voice to see how you can increase engagement, involvement, and academic motivation.

Michael Fullan, Joanne Quinn, & Joanne McEachen
Learn the right drivers to mobilize complex, coherent, whole-system change and transform learning for all students.

CORWIN
LEADERSHIP

Made in the USA
Columbia, SC
22 February 2023

12814162R00120